HINDU MYSTICISM

other recent books on similar topic

ENCYCLOPAEDIA OF TANTRA. in 5 Volumes
Edited by Sadhu Santideva *Bestseller*

ENCYCLOPAEDIA OF BUDDHIST TANTRA. in 5 Volumes
Edited by Sadhu Santideva

ENCYCLOPAEDIA OF INDIAN MYSTICISM. in 12 Volumes
Edited by Sadhu Santideva *Bestseller*

RITUALS AND PRACTICES OF TANTRA. in 3 Volumes
Gaurinath Sastri

THERAPEUTIC TANTRA.
The Power of Physical, Psychological, and Spiritual Healing
Edited by Gaurinath Sastri

INTRODUCTION TO TANTRA. in 2 Volumes
Gaurinath Sastri

Also Available . . .

THE HINDUS.
Encyclopaedia of Hinduism in 5 Volumes
Edited by Subodh Kapoor *Bestseller*

THE BUDDHISTS.
Encyclopaedia of Buddhism in 5 Volumes
Edited by Subodh Kapoor

ENCYCLOPAEDIA OF INDIAN HERITAGE. in 90 Volumes
A Descriptive Work of Indological Research in Philosophy, Religion, Sacred Literature, Society, Thought, Traditions, and Ancient Sciences.
Edited by Subodh Kapoor

HINDU MYSTICISM.
Studies in Vaisnavism and Tantricism in 2 Volumes
By Mahendra Natha Sarkar

Mysticism in Bhagavat Gita.
By Mahendranatha Sircar

HINDU MYSTICISM

[STUDIES IN VAIṢNAVISM AND TANTRICISM]

MYSTICISM OF THE TANTRAS

"Sri Ramkṛṣṇa Extension Lectures"

By
Mahendra Nath Sarkar

With a Foreword by
Sir N. N. Sircar, K.C.S.I.

PART II

COSMO PUBLICATIONS
2003 INDIA

HINDU MYSTICISM
SET IN 2 VOLUMES
This COSMO print 2003

ISBN 81-7755-739-4 (Set)
81-7755-741-6 (Volume 2)

Published by
MRS. RANI KAPOOR
for COSMO PUBLICATIONS Div. of
GENESIS PUBLISHING PVT. LTD.
24-B, Ansari Road, Darya Ganj,
New Delhi-110 002, INDIA
Tel.: 2328 0455; 2327 8779
Fax : 2324 1200

Printed at
Mehra Offset Press

PRELUDE

We are glad to present before the scholarly world and *Sādhakas,* Dr. Sircar's Mysticism of the Tantras, as the 2nd part of his Works on Hindu Mysticism. The first part of the book Vaiṣṇavic Mysticism was issued as the Śrī Kṛṣṇa Extension Lectures and this Part consisting of twelve lectures is issued as Śrī Rāma Kṛṣṇa Extension Lectures. Needless to say that Sri Ramakrishna, the sage of Modern Age had first communion with the Divine Mother through the Tantric Sādhanā. The lectures have been re-arranged into 24 chapters according to the subject-matters. It is also a happy coincidence that the book, the publication of which was long delayed due to various difficulties in securing paper etc. could be brought out on this auspicious day of the annual Pūjā Tithi of the Divine Mother.

It will not be out of place here to mention how such extension lectures were introduced. The Bhāratī Mahāvidyālaya, which was started a few years ago to be developed into one residential educational institution on the lines of ancient Gurukulas and Nālandā-Takṣaśilā Universities, on an extensive plot of land preferably by the Ganges within a few miles from the metropolis of Calcutta, wanted to organise extension lectures on different aspects of Indian Culture and Wisdom, prepared by scholars, eminent in their respective field of Studies, and named after the Prophets and Seers of the country. Accordingly several Series of such extension lectures named after Śrī Kṛṣṇa (on Vaiṣṇavism), Vyāsa (on the

Vedānta), Manu (on Social Sciences), Patañjali (on the Yoga), Lord Buddha (on Buddhism), Lord Mahāvīra (on Jainism) etc. were delivered and published in book-forms.

The Bhāratī Mahāvidyālaya has also been conducting several Pariṣats (Cultural Units) for researches into and propagation of different branches of Indian Literature. We are glad to announce that on this day, the Bhāratī Āgama Pariṣat is formed for similar researches into and publication of the Agam Literature—Tantras and Śaivāgama etc.

Dr. Sircar, who is well-known in the country and abroad as a great philosopher in its true sense, has now become specialised in the Mystical Tantric Sādhanā, and is therefore rightly entitled for discourses on the subject. He has tried his best to make the subject-matters intelligible to the general readers, through his lucid and simple style of expressions.

A few misprints have crept in in course of printing. The diacritical marks for Sanskritic words could not also be rigidly followed. They will be rectified in the subsequent edition.

It is expected that the publication will be well received by the scholars and *Sādhakas* of the Tāntric Path alike.

S. C. SEAL

Śyāmā-Pūjā Day, 1358 B.S.
Dated the 29th October, 1951
Gour Laha Street.
Calcutta—6

PREFACE

Mysticism in the Tantras is now published. It comes in succession to my other three books on Mysticism—Hindu Mysticism according to Upaniṣads, Mysticism in Bhagavat Gītā, Vaiṣṇavic Mysticism. I have tried to show how the mystical idea is gradually becoming dynamic and in the Tantras the dynamic side of life is in the forefront, and how it has been active in the understanding of life and its expression. The Tantras present the dynamic conception more forcefully, keeping intact the transmental sublimity along with immanental beauties of life. This is the most attractive side of the Tantras and it has supplied an attractive zeal to life. The Tantra therefore supplies the needful link in Indian thought and culture. It makes life attractive and beautiful, but the prevalent Tantricism is not being directed in the right way, for it does not see that the supramental is involved and immanent in the Subconscious and the Unconscious, and the Tantric inspiration has been directed to questionable channel. Tantracism can be revived to the benefit of Indian life and culture and in these days when there has been a great demand of the life force, the Cosmic Life and Will can be utilised to the advantage of the whole depressed humanity.

M. N. SIRCAR

To

The Divine Mother

CONTENTS

* Chap. VIII amalgamated with Chap. VII & IX.

CHAPTER I

INTRODUCTION

Before the revelations of the Soul, Time, Space, and Nature Shrink away (Emerson— The Over Soul).

The Tantras represent the collective wisdom of ages which unearths the composite nature of man and the forces functioning therein. They realise the ultimate truth of Transcendence and the liberation of the human mind from its restricted being and movement. The aspiration is manifestly evident of freedom from limited ways of life, of an assimilation of the cosmic consciousness, and acquaintance with the laws of its movement. The Tantras do not ignore the dynamic side of our existence; to ignore it is to leave full play to ignorance. To this position the Tantric inspiration is not committed. Naturally, the Tantras present a form of spiritual inspiration and a cast of thought which have their uniqueness. The uniqueness consists in their presenting the reality and the value of the dynamic aspect of existence which they called 'Sakti'. The Tantras retain the stress upon Transcendence of Being, but to this they add the eternal becoming as immanent in reality. The process is real, though in a certain sense it is transcended in the Absolute. But nowhere in the reality of being, becoming is denied, for it forms an intregal part of it. The Tantras are not limited to conceptual thinking and have not raised up a scaffolding of thought; their approach is through experience in all its grades, from the movement of the forces in the inanimate world, in the amoeba, up to the cosmical and supercosmical ranges. The attraction of the Tantras lies in this that they have not indulged in dialectic; by psychic intuition they discover the different layers of existence, individual and cosmic, and the forces active therein. Their importance in Indian thought lies in tracing out the fountain source of creative power and its formation in the different planes of existence. Truth is envisaged not through the forms of thought but through the evergrowing cosmic experience.

The Tantras do not go to the extreme of making the process a reality. The dynamic ingress or egress has a reference to a transcendent consciousness of being. That is the fixed point in our existence and consciousness which nothing can hide. They give their allegiance to the supreme Being and transcendent intuition as the ultimate fact not only of metaphysical but of spiritual significance. It is accepted as the primary datum and foundation of all spiritual experience. But the over-stress upon this fact and experience ignores the reality of becoming and the experiences revealed this way. The Tantras measure them not in a detached manner but in the full setting of integral existence. There is no meaning in denying what is so clearly evident and fills existence with its endless richness. There is a process of endless consciring. This consciring is not restricted to energy, life and mind but goes beyond them and it is difficult to determine its nature by mental concepts.

The Tantras follow the supreme revelation of the Word, of the ordering scheme immanent in its creative effort. No philosophy can be better than this, for it emerges out from intuitive realisation verified at each stage of experession by experience. It, therfore, does not suffer the uncertainties of intellectual efforts. Metaphysics is intellectual skill to map out the whole range of existence; but it invariably suffers limitation, for in the process of measuring the depths of existence, it builds up a scheme of thought and speculative scaffolding. It cannot enter into the heart of things and envisage their nature and essence. True metaphysics originates out of knowledge by identity, which is other than what is pursued in metaphysics *viz* reflection. The art of system-making is the sure process of intellectual satisfaction, but its narrowness becomes evident with new achievements in the widening of experience. The human intellect requires infinite patience in its search after the eternal, for as experience grows deep, facts, intensely interesting and supremely delicate, make their appearance and transfer the focuss of interest from the ordinary self-conscious seeking to the super-conscient revelation. And led by this urge the Tantras follow a path which opens the vistas of wider life and finer consciousness. Naturally here the envisagement of truth follows from the art of life, for art is the process and the method of unfoldment. The modulations of being can be so regulated that richer conscious life can be activated in us revealing supramental truths. This presupposes the plasticity of being, for truths are perceived directly and not discovered by thinking. Truth is immanent in life, and when life is finely attuned and nobly modulated, Truth is revealed. Life is harmony; its wider reaches and intensive depths can bring truth within easy reach. The Tantras follow naturally not the speculative method, but the immanent urge of being to grow in its wake. To be conscious fully and intensely is to approach truth intimately. It is unlike speculative thinking. It is acquaintance with the immanent spirit-force and consciousness which is at the root of all cosmic striving and impulse. The Tantras discover this *divine consciring* and pursue it, for it is not only the creative, constructive and additive force, but also the source of knowledge. It is what redeems us from the labryinth of experiences and invests us with cosmical feelings. Our conscious life is so complex that it is not impossible to draw our inspiration from one of its dominant notes and expressions and to build a construction and imperfect expression. Such has been the case when the analytical intellect has built up a philosophy. The integral functioning of consciousness has not been sympathetically understood. Inherent contradictions in our integral nature have been emphasised. Such must be the inevitable result of our truth-seeking when the knowledge by identity is displaced by ratiocinative thinking. Tantrik mysticism does not envisage Truth or Reality by cutting itself adrift from life, but by insisting upon life both in creative emergence and self-withdrawing process. In this process it can see the whole movement of life which gives better knowledge than understanding.

The Tantras by psychological analysis probe deeper. Their method is more psychological than logical. The psychological penetration exhibits the nature of ultimate becoming enfolded in Being. The Tantras do not dogmatise in any way, for their method is experience, and whatever conclusions they advance, they are based upon pure spiritual and psychological experince. It is really interesting to note how Tantric mysticism passes through fine aesthetic, psychic resonance, finally grasping the truth of both impersonal becoming and being. It realises transcendental and dynamical Being, with its twofold infinitude, (1) an unfettered quietus of being (2) a continuous becoming. The Tantras take cognisance of the composing forces in man, pychical, vital, mental, spriritual; and through a rare insight see their formations and functioning in life's setting. A theoretical philosophy is a natural sequence, for knowledge must be the fruition of psychological unfolding; but theoretical philosophy is not the aim, its value is not great in comparison with the direct experience achieved in the different layers of our being. The Tantras supply us with the richness of experience giving us the rare wisdom of the whole span of life in its graded expression and the poise of its being in every stage of its expression. They thus inspire us by offering the occult knowledge of the mysterious forces which are activated in us and exhibit the way to the still finer evolution of man in knowledge and spirituality. The attraction of the Tāntras lies here. This has been the secret of the Tantric inspiration and its strength. Philosophy or

Religion as intellectual illumination or spiritual aspiration does not carry us far to make our concrete life beautiful and quicken its evolution, unless the science to regulate the forces composing us is completly mastered to help our spiritual re-making.

CHAPTER II

TRANS-CONCEPTUAL CHRACTER OF REALITY

In Indian thought, specially in the Absolutistic Vedānta and in the Tantras, the ultimate reality is conceived as supra-logical. It is beyond the grasp of thought. When the mind thinks about it, it creates antinomies and contradictions. The mind thinks in relations, but the basic reality is beyond relations. It is non-relational. The usual attempt of characterising the ultimate existence as being—becoming, differentiating and then synthesising them is an intellectual process which the Tantras do not countenance. It is not possible to think of it as static or dynamic, though we are in the habit of doing so. The Tantras emphasise their integralness and characterise reality as "noumenal acting". Activity is not a mere category or concept, but refers to the transcendent creativity of the fontal power.

It is not the conscious will of the German metaphysics. It is not the transcendent subjectivity of the super-conscious. This transcendent activity is not internally determined and hence its expression is not controlled by logic. It is spontaneous. The transcendent activity is not a category of 'thought-determination' hence it is left free and indeterminate in its being and expression. Spirit is spontaneous activity. The divine consciring in the world process starts it, but it is difficult to determine its nature and method, for the whole process is at its root free and non-determinate. Divine consciring is not regulated by thought-forms, nor is its movement controlled by final ends. It is spontaneous in its movement and reason plays its part when it is objectified in the realm of ideas. But the essence and nature of the consciring proceed far beyond that. The world of ideas and concepts is true in a definite sphere, in the sphere of mentation, but reality exceeds that and operates in its own indeterminate way.

It is customary to characterise the basic reality as being-becoming. The initial situation is that which exists antecedent to the phase of developement. The being-becoming cannot be conceived separately, for it is ultimate. When the intellect thinks, it thinks of them separately. It is a limitation of the intellect. Becoming implies creativity, movement, world-rythm, violation and re-establishment of equilibrium; becoming understood in itself contrasts with being as "the metaphysical fall" from the poise and integrity of being. It is indeed possible to appraise the stages of becoming, and to determine the varied aspects in its cosmic consciring. But this is unsatisfactory as an enquiry into the whole of reality. The integral reality is being–becoming, no distinction can be drawn between them. Though there are phases of becoming,—creative, conservative, additive. destructive, it has also a phase of gravitating towards the centre and enjoying a poise in being before the time is ripe for another cycle of creative expression.

The supra-conceptual creativity or becoming is the primordial reality. This affirmation is almost identical with the affirmation of Whitehead. Still there is a distinction. In Whitehead the primordial reality acquires definiteness and rises into organism which represents a higher degree of truth. To Whitehead actuality is higher than potentiality, for there it gets its definite concrescence. Knowledge to him has always a definite meaning in a definite setting ; when there is the lack of definiteness and concrescence, nothing is left behind but a bare potentiality .... an indefinite consciring with no cosmic concrescence. Naturally to Whitehead actuality or creativity, is a higher degree of reality. The process of consciring is more real in the sense that it introduces definiteness, richness, in place of a bare potentiality. Tht metaphysical fall is to him more interesting, in as much as it is indispensable to creative advance. Nature "is the locus of organism in the progress of developement. The so-called locus of Whitehead is a poem, in which art transcending anything to which we aspire, is displayed on the cosmic scale". This art is involved in original creativity. There is no end of the creative concrescence. In the Tantras, there is the inverted movement towards the primordial creativeness and the original equilibrium. There is the poise beyond the creative rhythm, a lull in becoming. There is really an ascent along with a descent. This ascent is bent upon breaking the limitations of concepts and grasping the trans-conceptual creativity and its poise in its locus. Consciousness is to be freed from the limitations of concentration in subjects, from the limitations of creativity on the canvas of space and the loom of time ; the corner-stone of existence does not suffer the accidents of a definite and evanescent expression. The creative process is the process of concentration of the original becoming and its emergence into a definite order of cosmic consciring. The intial situation is lost sight of in its exhibition.

It is free from the subjective reference in knowledge and activity. Actuality represents potentiality in its concrete formation, but is not necessarily a phase of existence. Reality has no degrees. Emergents have. The greater universes are settings in the process of the emergence and creativity. Creativity by its effectiveness appears as dynamically more concrete and real; but the concreteness and the effectiveness are not necessarily the test of reality, it is true of variation or change but not of the dimensionless Existence. The conception of creative rhythm has its charm but it ignores the wideness of being. The Tantras evaluate reality as creative movement, becoming more and more concrete in emergence. but the creativity is linked up with the wideness of unfettered and unconcentrated being. There is the cyclic movement from and its withdrawal into the focus of being. The dynamic aspect of reality has been called Śaktī in the Tantras; and Māyā in the Vedanta. Śaktī brings out its energising chracter; Māyā, its limiting chracter. Śaktī or Māyā is the principle of individuation. This principle of individuation is the principle of self-limitation. This self-individuating principle, according to theTantras (of the Kashmere school,) is inherent in the ultimate reality,—Śiva. To the Vedānta it is seemingly inherent in the Absolute. This marks out the difference between them. The Tantras regard tht world to be the creative play of Śiva. The Vedānta also regards it as creative play, which has empirical or even pragmatic significance but no real or metaphysical import. The Tantras attach real significance to the creative movement. It is not illusion even as appearance. It is self-expression (Svātantryābabhāsa) of the Absolute and is real. The Tantras have stressed the dynamic aspect of existence and traced the evolution of mind, life and matter out of the original creative Śakti, centred in transcendent Absolute. The wheel of creation moves eternally. There are cycles when the creative force is withdrawn into the absolute background, where it enjoys the occasional poise before the start of a new cycle for expression. This creative will in the Tantras is more than the urge of life, more than the practical reason (or will). It is the principle of cosmic formation, the Absolute in its creative consciring.

The Tantras avoid two extremes, the absolute distinction and separation between the creative principles of change and individuation as transcendentally non-existent. It recognises the principle of consciring as one with the Supreme Existence. ("Only when united with Śakti has Siva the power to create, without her the Śiva cannot even stir" —Ānanda Laharī, Verse I).

The theory of causation is not confined to the phenomenal world. Change is self-contradictory in Absolutist metaphysics, for the reality, it affirms, is not a process. But change supposes a process. The Vedānta attempts to make a synthesis of the scientific view of causation with the Metaphysical Absolute by recognising that the Absolute contains the principle of efficiency and concrete consciring which it ultimately transcends. Causation is a scientific concept in the phenomenal world. But its notion is not made clear unless the potential creativity is realised besides the succession of phenomena. This potential consciring is the root of the change. Hence creative causation is ascribed by the Vedānta to the Absolute. It is no surface change in the phenomenal universe which keeps every detail of phenomena hung up in vacuum ; the urgency of thought arises to trace out the *creative consciring* to reality. But causation is true of the world of creative consciring, in the order of actuality but not in the order of reality. Actuality and Reality represent two orders. The Vedānta accepts the category of causality in the order of reality when it is viewed in the setting of actuality. This reference disappears in the setting of the Absolute Reality. The heart of Reality is more than its expression in creativity. Thought grasps the Synthesis of Reality and actuality by conceiving actuality as creative expression of Reality.

At a certain stage of our knowledge, prior to the final illumination, this synthesis is necessary in order that nothing outside the reference to the Absolute can be conceived. This is the limit of scientific thinking, which metaphysical thinking modifies by showing that it is preliminary to final, trans-empirical conception of reality. The Vedānta at this stage denies causation and change by withdrawing the individuality or specificness of changes which becomes inconsistent with its identity and sameness. The absolute transcends the becoming or change.

The Tantras almost agree with the Vedānta, but they do not go to the same length and conceive creative consciring as fundamental to reality. The absolute is trans-empirical, but it positively contains the consciring principle. It denies the phenomenal theory of causation, but accepts the dynamic theory. The Tantras do not extend relational thinking to the ultimate reality, which is really beyond all thinking. And therefore it will not be strictly cogent to regard the supreme principle in relational terms. It is not being-becoming. It is being that becomes. It is consciring reality. The logical categories are introduced when the consciring process starts. Before that it is indefinite and supra-conceptual. Hence no ideas of causation can be introduced into it. (Śivecchhayā parā Śakti Śivatatwaikagatā) Abhinava Gupta in his Pratyabhijña Hṛdayaṃ accepts a non-differential state of being. This non-differentiation is not the transcendent Brahman of the Vedānta, for the creative consciring is to him real. The ultimate reality is integral, not by denying but by assimilating the consciring. To distinguish his transconceptual system from the Vedantic view point, he calls it Parama Ādvaita. It does introduce the integral character of existence by completely assimilating the consciring activity. It is an integral awareness which does not admit of relations, and naturally transcends the distinction and relation of a logical system. Abhinava Gupta is clear on this point, though he characterises the ultimate existence as Śunyam. The mental ways of appraising things are not prevalent here and naturally it is devoid of conceptual content. The difference between the Vedantic monism and the Parama-advaita form of Tāntricism is a matter of emphasis on identity. In both there is the displacement of initial ignorance, which introduces differential concepts of Actuality and Reality, and the recognition of the self as identical with the Trans-conceptual reality; recognition, because there is temporary forgetfulness. The recognition is the recovery of lost ground. In the one it establishes the dynamic identity in which the recognitive process is ceaselessly active. In the other it gives way to the established fact beyond recognition. Recognition is the intermediate step towards the final realisation. In the Pratyabhijña school recognition is assimilated as an element in the immediate dynamic awareness. This makes the distinction clear between the position of the Advaitists and the Trantricists. (Kāshmere Śaivaism). Immediacy of awareness is presented in both. Naturally no relational or conceptual sense can subsist anywhere, for the aspiration is to rise above the conceptual limitation of thought and to realise the identity with the basic existence or reality.

The Tantras do not accept the Pariṇāmavāda of the Sāṁkhya. No transformation of the Absolute reality can be conceived. It is possible for the Sāṁkhya to accept this, because of the ultimate dualism of a transcendent reality and creative principle. The Tantras maintain the emergence to be really expression, projection of the

Absolute out of itself and as projections it is non-different from it.

There can be two forms of emergence or projections. The one holds that the emergence or projection is illusion. It is objective, but is not the basic existence. The other holds that emergence is real projection. It is creative expression. It may withdraw again into the ultimate reality in the state of dynamic equilibrium. But it is not illusion. The individuating principle is non-different from the basic reality, which in association with the creative will assumes its initial nature. The Tantras reconcile the unitive and the creative nature of the Absolute. The reality of the creative act is accepted fully and naturally. The Tantras do not favour the theories of the world as imagination or the world as idea. Both of them introduce 'the subjectivity of the creative act', which the Tantras cannot accept. Ideas are, according to the Tantras, really forces or projections of will. Will is the primary fact, ideas are derivatives of will. Ideas are mental forms and when we speak of the world as the objectification of ideas, the evident supposition is that the world is a mental creation. Will is the primary energy, the primitive *spiritual act,* which takes the definite forms of ideas when the world of not-self emerges. Ideas have a reference to it, will has no such reference. The spiritual act is *free* and is not determined by 'the other'. The primitive creative act takes definite lines of expression. These are objectifications and definite formations in the world of ideas. In affirming this the Tantras do not accept that the will or the original spirit-act is an unconscious force. It is the spirit or Reality in its creativity ; since self-consciousness implies a meditating process, this spirit-act or intuition is not self-conscious ; though it may attain this at a cosmic stage of expression. It is not unconscious. The word "unconscious" has dubious implications. It may imply the absence of consciousness or that which is beyond the bounds of the self-conscious. The Tantras reject the former, they accept the latter. Consciousness has a phase which transcends all relativity. Will is the consciousness of spirit in its creativity. This creativity introduces the order of self and not-self, but creativity really transcends it. It has no reference to subjectivity. for this naturally implies the illusiveness of creation or even of the creative act which the Tantras deny. It is really transcendental creativity, a spontaneous free act, which bifurcates (as the Pratyabhijñā Hṛdayaṃ points out) into a cosmic subject and a cosmic object (Adam and Idam). There is no relational import in this height of existence. The primordial substance is therefore called 'Śūnyam' which indicates its transcendence more than its content. The world of space and time is the objectification of this creative act and is not the creative matrix of the universe without reference to it. Eventually the subject becomes limited to finite consciousness and finite individuality.

The creative advance is attended with limited knowledge and activity, the consciring in its definite form has its centricity and location. It becomes, therefore, associated with its locus. The centralisation becomes more and more definite with creative advance. God is the first concrete formation in the process of consciring, it has introduced the world of creative ideal and values distinct from the primordial consciring which is not regulated by them. Personality or personal experiences and the sense of good are definite formations which are husbanded in the conceptual expression. A formation in advance may appear as higher emergence, which it is not. It may add to creative diversity, and emotional novelty, but that which constitutes its uniqueness and novelty keeps it separate from supreme existence and its indefinite being and consciring. There is the oscillation in being to pass from its indefinite to definite formations. There is the counter-movement to break the centralised movement and consciousness to pass into unfettered being and equilibrium.

The Tantras maintain two kinds of subjectivity in the finite individual and the cosmic individual. The subjectivity is the sense of a concerntrated being with its definite expression in knowledge and will. It is really the definite expession of the primordial consciousness as exhibited through determinate creativity and through history. The definite formations have emergence, continuity and lapse. The cosmic individual has the inherent power of projecting itself into the different forms by which it controls the cosmic process. These forms are not to be supposed as different from the basic cosmic subject; they are its projections. The projections to us have distinct beings and forms; but in reality they are ideal expressions of the same reality. The projections have acquired an individuality by the functions they perform, but their individualities are not absolute. These projections are the cosmic powers.

The same subject, when it is focussed through individual psychism, is the finite individual. The finite individual takes definite expression in accordance with the psychic formation of its being. The cosmic and the individual subjects have no other difference besides the magnitude of their being and power. They are not categorically different. Since the concentration is not absolute, the individual can rise to an immeasureable height of being, but can never forsake his individual concentration, or attain the height of cosmic being. But by spiritual and psychic discipline it is possible for the individual to attain a dynamic identification with the cosmic power and intelligence and occasionally feel the pulse of cosmic creativity; but this dynamic identification is a temporary possession.

In the Pratyabhijña School recognition of identity is the intermediate step to realisation. But there is the constant awareness in the heart of reality beyond recognition.

CHAPTER III

SCIENCE AND ART IN THE TANTRAS.

Mysticism, since it reflects the whole of life, is at once science, art and philosophy. This is especially true of the Tantras. As science it advances the fine psychology of our make-up, probing deeper into its formations unearthing the forces that array themselves in the different strata of existence from the physical to the spiritual. The knowledge of the forces, their inter-connexion and inter-dependence are necessary to set and establish definite tunes in our being and to give them a spiritual tone. The Tantras study the vital, the physiological and the psychic composition of our being, not to understand their individual nature, but to reflect their bearing upon the total nature of our being. These forces are studied not in isolation, but in the context of our total being. The interest is concrete; the forces are studied not in the abstract, but in a concrete setting especially in their influence upon the interest and expression of life.

Naturally the scientific analysis of the forces can not give the final satisfaction. It must be shown how they unite to serve the higher ends of life and spirit, how they become the media through which the spirit can re-act upon the mental, the vital, the physiological and the physical forces of our being. Spirit is the ultimate reality, but in its descent it suffers in expression and appears as mind, life and matter. Hence in mystical life, it is necessary to note the complex make-up of man, in order that his whole being may be brought under the direct influence of spirit to recover consciousness in every part of our being and directly to put it under the influence and inspiration of spirit. The mysticism of the Tantras has, therefore, this speciality that it is the study of the concrete man. It does never forget this central point; it traces the connexion between the concrete man and the whole universe in its fine and gross aspect, and traces out the correspondence between the microcosm and macrocosm. Man represents the universe in miniature and reflects the centre of cosmic existence. When this is forgotten, the intrinsic interest is lost. Man is studied in a cosmic setting. The universe is an organic existence, man is the prototype of this organic existence.

This correspondence advances a finer analysis of forces composing our being and points to the direct relation between the inner and the outer not only on the surface but in their deeper levels of consciring. Subtle forces array themselves The mysticism that is presented in the Tantras has to its advantage this wide knowledge of astral energies, that silently give shape to our psychic and vital being. These astral forces are in direct connexion with the higher forces of intelligence and spirit. The Tantras make a searching analysis of the seen and the unseen forces active in us. They localise them in different parts of our being and find out the most sensitive parts where their presence and functions can be directly felt. This is the scientific aspect that the Tantras present.

This wide knowledge of the subtle force has its bearing upon the art of life. This art essentially is the modulation of the life-forces in a manner which endows us with rare knowledge and power. The perfect art of life is to receive and harmonise all the forces in us, and to remove all obscurities. The former establishes the finer tune, the latter sets aside the disturbing forces. The conflicts and incongruities are discordant to the spiritual existence. By the superior knowledge of the forces in our nature, by the fine modulation of our being the Tantras make it responsive to the finer forces functioning there, and make them active in us, so that life may grow in beauty, harmony, power and transcendence. This art is the most difficult of all. It is the art of re-orienting our being which can make us feel and receive the inrush of the spirit force. There is an equilibrium in our being, which is, at times disturbed by the immanent urge of growth. Every higher stage in evolution restores the equilibrium. The spiritual art in the Tantras, advances the spiritual evolution. It keeps up the "divinity of measure". At every step of evolution and expression this divinity of measure is better established in as much as it gets access to the wider harmony of being. In the intermediate stages the harmony and the equilibrium are disturbed for the attainment of the wider harmony, The divinity of measure is again restored in a higher plane. The spiritual art invigorates our being in all its parts, and throws light even in the remotest parts of our being to rejuvenate them and transform them and to establish in them the divine tune. The greatest art is the transformation of our nature. It is really re-creative, re-shaping our original crude impluses of nature into diviner shapes and beauteous forms. It discovers the archtypes and remoulds after them. This is why spirituality is so much valued. Evolution is carried to a higher status, when the archtypal forces can be made active in us.

The Tantras advance the art of spiritualising the whole of life by discovering the central being and by connecting it with the fountain of life, light, knowledge and power, invigorating our whole being with spiritual force. It vibrates the deeper chords of our being in order that the most potent spiritual force may be awakened and activated in us. Science gives the knowledge of the forces, art discovers their integration in the total setting and uses them to establish creative harmony and perfect poise in order that wider amplitude in consciousness may be obtained. In this sense the Tantras are the greatest spiritual discipline to evoke the finer ryhthms passing into wide stretches of knowledge and consciousness. The Tantras do not indulge in abstract thought: the advance in spiritual realisation at every step is followed by the concrete adaptation to life, especially in the moulding of our concrete being. The formation of the concrete being is imperatively necessary. Truth is not only to be thought, but to be assimilated and made dynamic in us. The spiritual realisation has to present not only the abstract truths in the setting of life but to assimilate them in the life process. The hidden forces and potentialities attain supramental heights of expression and evolution. The divinity of measure overtakes our being. The higher scale of our concrete being is crossed. Spiritual art gives divine philosophy or wisdom. It can easily appraise the different formations of our being, their setting, and their emergence from and withdrawal into the central being and the final freedom of consciousness from the turns and twists of our life and being. Spirituality establishes definite harmonies in the different parts of our being, revealing the Great Truth of the ineffable Silence, which is the supreme fact of existence. Thus it gives a kind of philosophy not halting at each stage with definite experience and attempting partial constructions, but entering straight into the heart of reality, transcending every partial revelation, the half truths and the side-lights. It gives supramental lights and truths and avoids mentation regarding them. Where the light of revelation reaches, the need of reflection does not arise. The Tantras develop the power of seeing Truth and their art is so to equip our faculties that the direct envisagement of Truth may be possible. The art is here revelation.

Art and Philosophy go together in the Tantras. Art is creative. It is also revelative. It gives the definite spiritual attitude which can easily quicken the forces dominant in us and make them serviceful to realisation. The Tantras rely upon it to vouchsafe divine wisdom. Philosophy is, here, the envisagement of the complete truth directly and immediately without the long process of ratiocination. The spiritual art modulates our psychic being presenting the wider and finer experiences and the composition of the forces regulating our complex being. It probes deeper, and one not accustomed to it naturally is not in a position to correctly understand and promptly evaluate the subtle forces which the Tantras discover and to follow their internal and external correspondence. The Tantras give an occult art and estoric philosophy—a perfect seeing of the forces operating in creation. In the final envisagement of truth which transcends both the scientific deciphering of forces and the artistic modulations of being, they give profound knowledge of being and becoming and endow us with rare intuitions and divine imagination which displace our limited vision and inspire us with the power of spiritual construction. The superb beauty of the Tantric wisdom lies in acquainting us with the spiritual architecture of the world, the immanent radiant forces and the divine consciring in the heart of existence. The divine sapentia includes within it all the formative forces, the creative harmonies the wider synthesis as well as the inscrutable silence and ineffable peace. Transcendence and creativeness are blended in the life of spirit and the Tantras take cognisance of both; and hence in the art if life, the Tantras exhibit the deeper insight into spiritual life. To fix the spiritual ideal and objective to Transcendence is really to forget the charm of life in the spirit. The Spirit is appreciated most in its dignity and beauty when it is exhibited in its polarisation and its linking us of Heaven and Earth, and it is intuited not in its sublime silence, but in its most meaningful expression through the concrete formation of life in every plane of its expression. Spiritual life, besides its transcendent sublimity, has its expression in Count Keyserling's phrase "terristrial gravity". The Tantras, in emphasising the creative expression of spirit, have introduced an additional charm in life and have discovered spiritual meaning in life's urges and spiritual beauty in life's formations. It gives a new vesture to life's creative urge, which appears profounder because of the spiritual significance it manifests.

The exquisite artistic display is exhibited when the spirit releases the sleeping creative forces and activates them in all the strata of our being, mental, vital, and sub-vital and ultimately infuses them with higher inspiration and starts a new re-orientation of our being. It is indeed a fine art to make these forces active in order that Heaven may counter-act upon Earth and gradually instil into it its influence. This is the greatest spiritual venture, the finest expression of the creative act of spirit. The spirit cannot allow the total suspension of the creative activity and naturally it must discover the force which can help to remove the obstruction of matter in order that the creative expression in life may be impregnated with spirit. Occult science and occult art go together. The knowledge of the forces suggests the clue to their regulation. Life emerges in its dignity and beauty. Nothing crude and ugly can be left in it. Movement becomes graceful, being becomes transparent and luminous. Man is exhibited as a supreme specimen of the divine art in creation, angelic in form and movement.

CHAPTER IV

RELIGION AND PHILOSOPHY IN THE TANTRAS

Religion is closely associated with art. Religion is integrative, art creative. It is self-immersion. The religious aspiration is the yearning after 'the visitation of the living God'. The spiritual life has two movements, (1) to free itself from the cob-web of the mazes of life, instinctive, vital, and mental, and (2) to establish a direct connexion between our central being and the fountain head of existence. This is followed by direct infusion in our being of spiritual charges. A supreme puissance seizes our being. Religious consciousness implies the sense of the infinite, the temporary dropping of the creative expressions and the self-loss in the Eternal silence and peace, the recovery of the lost paradise. But this is followed by the descent of spirit in all the parts of our existence, transmuting them and calling to service the hidden forces. The Spirit seizes our whole being. Its call is imperious. It brooks no challenge. It demands allegiance from the complete being in order that its balming influence may scatter itself everywhere making a better and a wider expression possible. The divine art exhibits the working of forces, their beauties, their rhythms, their harmonies, in order that man may outgrow his partial and limited expressions of an unillumined personality. Religion inspires art. The religious art informs this new creative power. The architectonic form and inspiration emerge from a subtle height.

This creative expression in spiritual life does not take away from it the grace of a divine union, for once the spirit seizes, it never leaves its charge. The spirit has in it a creative necessity. Naturally the two movements run concurrently. Spirit maintains the easy flow of creation along with its luminous silence. Its expression becomes spontaneous because it makes the instrument soft and plastic.

The Tantras lay emphasis upon indentification with the creative will. The personal will is raised to the supreme height and power, not by denying its concreteness and definite functioning, but by reinforcing it by the supreme will.

This identification is the natural sequence of our spiritual quest, for the spirit shakes off its loneliness and helplessness and the field of its limited play by affilliating itself to the centre of divine light and power. Spirituality has no meaning, far less any charm, if there is not some form of identification with supreme puissance and existence. This identification may be complete or partial, and static or dynamic: but none can disown it. This is its unique attraction and promise. The greatest attraction in spirituality lies in not acquainting us with the supreme truth, but with the supreme puissance and felicity, for the spirit is essentially that. The appeal of religion lies that way. Truth is the quest of philosophy, puissance and felicity of religion. And this becomes a permanent acquistion by identifing our being with the supreme felicity. This identification can alone make the promise fulfilled, by removing the sense of separateness. Naturally all religions make the promise of wider being, a richer and finer delight as the supreme goal of our existence. The Tantras recover the life-impulse in spirituality, for they are ever awake to the spiritual formation in creative expression; they have not ignored the creative expression of spirit in the different layers of existence and take supreme interest in their terrestrial functioning, without losing its reference to its central locus in the transcendence. Hence the Tantras can see the values of all forms of spiritual expression from its most rudimentary to its loftiest forms. The opening of the wide amplitude of becoming makes it possible for the Tantras to embrace the spiritualistic tendencies expressed in every form of religious inspiration and this explains the rather apparently incongruous position of them in affiliating the contradictary conceptions of spirituality. The Tantras do not go by the rigid intellectual formations, and in the setting of life they find no contradiction in varied spiritual forms and thought-casts. This acceptance of life-impulse and will-force and their final reference to the supreme will and puissance give a special grace and character to the mysticism of the Tantras, for it does not go by the spirit of rejection. Its spirit of acceptance is inspired by insight into the truer and diviner nature of the moving impulses and their formations. They can immediately see the archetypal setting, the aesthetic beauties, and moral sublimities in the creative expression and their spiritual significance and meaning. The vital, aesthetic, and artistic impulses acquire true meaning when they are envisaged as spiritual expressions and spiritual formations. This lends an additional grace to them which they lack in their normal presentations. The Tantras do not encourage the escapist mentality, usually associated with religion. The Tantras. fully alive to this spirit of this artist, realise the great consummation not by the rejection but by the conquest of life, by entering sympathetically into its subtler course, and finally discovering the responsiveness to the graces of life.

Here is the supreme effort of the Tantras : to trace out all the creative forces, to acquaint us with the joy in creation, to bring out the supreme felicities of spirit in its blissful expressions, and finally to pass into the transcendent. The Tantras read the whole texture of our being first hand through psychic insight and divinise all the forces that are working there.

The Tantras give full satisfaction to religious consciousness and pass eventually into philosophic wisdom. Religion inspires moral, aesthetic, beautitude by focussing our being in God and inspiring communion with Him. According to the Tantras, it releases fine occult forces from the different psychic centres of our being. It moves hidden forces of our nature into creative channels and widens our consciousness to embrace reality in its transcendental dignity and immanental sublimity. Religion saturates our whole being, in all its strata, with freshness and fervour. The religious consciousness is not an occasional attitude of divine fellowship. It is the re-making of man in such a way that his entire being responds to the spiritual urge and revives it through all the grades of his consciousness. It really attunes our being to the Divine chime. The original impulses are thus beautified, and nothing remains in man which is not divinised. Religion is not a temporary sentiment, a passing feeling. It establishes the permanent habit of God in man. The vital rejuvenation and quickness, the emotional intensity and grace, the suppleness and the plasticity of our being are all afforded by religious consciousness. The excess of emotional expression and the concentration thereupon have been the cause of separating spiritual enthusiasm from philosiphic wisdom This comes from confining life impulse to religion and thought-impulse to philosophy.

The Tantras do not entertain such a division, for thought is the cast of life and is immanent in life. Spirituality accepts its help and instrumentality in so far as it reflects light on life-impulses and helps their adjustments. Ultimately religion is the expression of the spirit and its yearning after the enduring and the eternal. This impulse is the greatest in man, and therefore religious consciousness ultimately must overcome emotional concentration and pass into the still higher reaches of rarefied consciousness in its sublime silence and transcendence. The Tantras do not lose sight of this height of spiritual experience. It is true wisdom, where the process of becoming and its synthetic setting are withdrawn in the inscrutable Being. Religion there passes from a devotional and emotional experience and from the concordant movement of will to transcendent and serene peace.

Religion ordinarily is so much associated with life-impulse that it is not easy to see the wisdom of this conclusion. The Tantras more than any scriptures of the Hindus have acknowledged the supremacy of life-impulse and the creative will and consciring but they have not been slow to recognise the indubitable supremacy of transcendence and silence to creative impulse and readily accepts it as a far superior spiritual consummation. To ignore this is to ignore the completeness of spiritual-life, to fail to recognise the supreme puissance and transcendence of the spirit.

The Tantras do not agree with those who identify religion exclusively with the fine dynamism of the spirit for they have the deeper intuition of luminous silence behind the creative urges of the spirit. The Spirit conscires, but it does not change. It remains what it is, even when it individuates. It is what it is. Spiritual consciousness is the acceptance of the transcendent truth by the unfolding of our psychic nature. It acquaints it with the progressive realisation of spiritual experiences in the path of ascent. The stretched out, graded, striving of the biological evolutionist, the many-sided universe of the psychical relativist, the space-time manifold of realist philosophy ignored by the religious mind has not been ignored by the Tantras. They have been grasped, affiliated to the supreme reality known in religious experience. They are true in reference to their order and are accepted as presenting partially the blissful consciring. Naturally religious life outgrows them in its aspiration after the fuller and finer consciring and is, therefore, a finer emergence in which the partial presentations are accomodated and integrated.

The spiritual path is laid up with intermediate grades and exquisite glimmers, but it leads straight on to the supreme truth if the pursuit is not checked by the pleasing and engrossing experiences of the partial presentations. The Tantras integrate and affiliate experiences in a systematic setting.

Art and religion with which the creativeness and harmony of life are associated cannot carry the same privilege ; art cannot, by its very nature of creative expression, religion to a degree can, when it foregoes the emotional graces, and takes its cue from the higher planes of consciousness. It then overcomes the emotional delight and the ecstatic exaltation and proceeds to the wise passiveness whence it enjoys the supreme puissance of transcendent truth and calm, equable delight. The religious attitude is dominant in the Tantras, there is an approach to Truth through the psychic opening, and not through intellectual dissertation and intellectual intuiton. But this spiritual aprcach through psychic intuition does not necessarily confine our spiritual gaze to its ordinary limitations of a personal or cosmical feeling and relation; but carries it through finer spiritual perspectives to the realisation of the absolute. This is the final experience. It ranges beyond the occult experiences, the delightful harmonies, the modulations of our being. There is evidently a difference in the nature and the character of these experiences and they belong to the different orders of existence. The psychic intuitions acquaint us with the spiritual potencies, and formations, enriching our being with exquisite experiences, but they cannot go beyond. Spirituality here takes a different turn from the quick flashes of being to its mysterious silence. It is the experience of the basic reality, and the realisation is characterised not by any special emphasis on any side of our conscious life. Spirituality at this height is unique. It finds no expression either in Art, or in Thought, or in Occult experience. Life impulse cannot be moulded at this height. It is this suprapersonal Experience which is the meeting point of Religion and Philosophy in the Tantras. Religion is a scheme of valuation of the forces of existence relative to their satisfactoriness or agreeableness; but with superior inspiration, this subjective character of religion is changed into a trans-subjective character; the very spiritual inspiration, if rightly followed throughout, exhibits the impulse to transcend personal feelings, however intensive and agreeable. Properly conceived, religion is not the estimate if Reality in reference to a subjective attitude, it has in it the urge to appraise it itself beyond the feelings it produces in personal setting. Religion in its supreme effort appraises Reality in a super-personal sense. It then becomes identical with Philosophy. In Indian thought, specially in Tantricism and Vedantism (Advaita), religion has this implication.

CHAPTER V.

THE SPIRITUAL OBJECTIVE

The Tantras present a wide field of spiritual realisation, since they accept the process of ascent which reveals the cosmic powers and the wide reach of immediate experiences accompanying them. These indeed are rich and absorbing experiences and the Tantras lay not a little emphasis upon them. They start a spiritual tuning of being. Each little shade of experience produces a wave of blissful feeling. There is infinite variety, all moving to higher rhythms of consciousness and to the higher expressions of being. These experiences are concrete, having definite meaning and expression. They are welcome because of the freedom they allow from the earthly setting of life and the acquaintance they establish with the spiritual setting. The Tantras thus afford us elevating experiences, allowing admission into the subtler range of consciousness and existence. These are still limited experiences ; they may be subtle and finely consciring yielding fresh feilds and pastures new for experiences. The consciring is expressed in definite ways at the different ladders of being. Hence the realisation must be concrete at certain stage of spiritual unfoldment. There is every chance of indentifying oneself with these expressions and of continuing forever in a definite universe of realisation. The spiritual experiences are so removed from ordinary experience and they are so subtle that the definite conscirning cannot be mastered unless our being is finely responsive. In these experiences 'knowledge is co-relative with the existent.' In psychic intuition, there is definite formation; the knowledge thereof is direct and immediate. A sudden flash and appearance with its wide luminosity and transparence characterise it and the sense of a holiness and a transfigured consciousness is all that is left to us. These concrete experiences introduce a new horizon of spiritual consciousness, quickly vibrative and enjoyable in the extreme, exhibiting the intermediate zones. They indicate a definite advance in the spiritual tremor of being. This advance really acquaints us with the waves of cosmic life, which grows wider as it recedes from the definite setting of life. Far beyond is the 'cloud of unknowing', the quietus of Being in which every concrete experience, however subtle is overcome. The consciring is suspended, a level reached beyond *truth* whereon there is no knowledge of a correlative existence as Plato puts it. The experience passes into the indefinite, which we can indicate as 'the bliss-lit silence', beyond the cosmic and transcendent harmonies. The Tantras acknowledge the demand of a holier and a finer expression of every part of our being, and naturally they recognise, along with the bliss-lit silence, the concrete spiritual transformation. Personality gets fullest expression when the conflicting forces covering its super-human character are withdrawn. Thus the Tantras allow the evolution of our being to a higher stage, and its delicate expression and formation endowed with richness in intuitive wisdom, spontaneous movement and graceful harmonies. Every step in advance removes the barrier of our being and invites greater freedom and wider being and the creative concrescence gets more embracive expression. The inertia of our being is removed, and a new life-force is released. Indeed, it has been the great effort in the Tantras, not to submit to the limitations of nature and to find out a way of escape, by the process of discrimination, between spirit and nature, but to take full cognisance of nature's forces and to de-naturalise them by a superior force. Nature is there, by our blind acceptance and refusal to measure the true height of our being. It is the confession of ignorance. This ready acceptance of the solicitations of nature is a movement born of ignorance which causes polarisation of being into spirit and nature. Hence the Tantras are concentrated upon depolarising the original polarisation in order to get mastery over it. Each step towords depolarisation proves the strength of the spirit and its contol over nature and its capacity to transform and trans-figure it. The appeal of the concrete spiritual life lies in this that it demonstrates the divine consciring at every step and affords the joy of the re-affirmation of spirit over matter and its subtle expression through life-force and life-impulse.

In this connexion it should be known that there is the central being in man, the being remains inoperative in us. The objective and the subjective minds are so pre-occupied with the impression from the outer or inner being, that they do not allow us to go still deeper. The subjective mind is filled up with its forces and unless an even detachment be carried out. it is difficult to get still deeper access and to come in touch with the central being. The one great indication of this is that our being gets then a direct access into the cosmic consciousness and our knowledge nas no obstruction. The subjective psychology gives the theory of the unconscious, where all the hidden forces of our nature are conserved but the central being exceeds both the conscious and the unconscious. Our personality with its hidden and expressed powers stands revealed before it. When the central being begins to function in us we are lifted from the limited and obscure visions, either of the objective or of the subjective mind. They appear as distant though naturally seem to be most intimate with us. They represent indeed the outer surface, the most limited part of our being. The central being is luminious directly from the cosmic consciousness. The Tantras lift the veil from the central being. The central being receives direct oscillation of the divine life; and if the intrusion from the subjective and the objective mind can be suspended the inspiration can be received continuously and spontaneously. This central being is the direct intermidiary between our person and the cosmic being. It can receive the radiant forces and reflect them on the unconscious and the conscious. It can throw the divine effulgence in the remotest corner of our being, the conscious and the unconscious. When the light streams through the central being, both the conscious and the unconscious are suffused with the divine light. Man becomes the child of light. Here is concealed the divine wisdom, the divine life and divine power. Human evolution has not proceeded far enough to put us in direct touch with the central being. The evolution is furthered when its contact is well established, for through this the new moulding force can be active and operative, reason is displaced by intuition, doubt by faith. limited vision by cosmic imagining. Man sees thecosmic consciring and feels its active formations through the universal existence. The central being can alone put us in touch with cosmic consciring and redeem us from the slow, wonted ways of knowledge and life.

CHAPTER VI.

SPIRITUALITY AND OCCULTISM

To be spiritual is to be fully conscious in all the parts of being, spiritual life is engrossing because of this promise. It establishes the wideness of consciousness and makes it constantly vibrative and alive in our intergal being, in the centre as well as in the circumference. To grow more and more intensively and extensively conscious is the supreme privilege of spiritual life. Our consciousness does not stand at the same pitch everywhere. The promise of spiritual life lies in making every part of our being intensively conscious and equally luminous.

Philosophers speak of the height of spiritual realisation as *sub-specie aeternitatis*. It is supra-conceptual experience, the significance and the import of which are not properly felt and understood unless we grow conscious to full height. The mind cannot comprehend its full significance. The finest mental effort is exhibited in the synthetic vision of reality in its harmonious setting. But it does not signify the full of spiritual realisation. The vision is still mental, it is the expression of the higher mind verging on intuitive consciousness. Still it is indeed poor in comparison with the higher strtches of super-mental consciousness. To be conscious has, therefore, an implication in spiritual life different from its implication as ordinarily understood.

To be conscious is to be conscious in our supra-conscious as well in our sub-conscious being. To be conscious is to feel the whole of existence with its vivyfying spirit. The present consciousness of man is focussed in a centre. Even in its limitation consciousness is a mystery, for its full working cannot be completely visualised. The mystery becomes indeed great when its full depth is fathomed. And yet, there is the constant urge in man to accomplish this apparently impossible task. This demand is the demand of his being.

With this calling true spirituality starts. Divine wisdom or philosophy consists not in analysing the thought-concepts and in starting a world theory therefrom, but really in traversing the whole range of conscious life, especially in its wider reaches. It is not the intellectual glimpse of the unknown and the invisible; it is the vivid realisation of the subtle movements of conscious life in its transcendental dignity and immanental sublimity. It is the intimate acquaintance with the life of the spirit in its transcendence and with its full play through terrestrial expression, through the cosmic life and mind. It is not vague sentimentality. It is knowledge. It is wisdom. It gives knowledge of the forces that function not only in us, but in all the planes of existence. The Tantras are occult science and philosophy at the same time. To the divine sapentia nothing can remain hidden either within us or outside us. It is this consummation that spirituality seeks, and naturally with spirituality is usually associated the hidden treasure of knowledge which cannot be revealed in any other way.

This unceiling of nature's secret forces introduces occultism. Occultism is the knowledge of the subtle forces functioning in us, which the human mind with all its scientific skill has not been able to fathom. And naturally it is supposed as something imaginary and fanciful. Its inaccessible nature cannot dismiss its reality. It is sure in existence, positive in functioning. The evolution of man in spirituality gives him the intimate knowledge of the invisible and marevellous forces that operate in him and nature, and endows him with supra-natural powers, and supra-natural wisdom. Divine wisdom gives divine powers. Life manifests beauteous movements, its indomitable forces, its unbounded creative expressions, above all its divine character and endless possibilities, its contribution to ethereal blessedness and happiness in this very existence. It is not imagination. It is experience, it is actuality.

Spirituality has long been associated with occultism and the way in which these powers are misused by the untrained novice and the initiate has made it the objcet of frontal attack. But the privilege which it affords, can be construed into a holier power in the hands of the adepts. That is a point in applied occultism. It is enough to know that occultism is not to be condemned, because it is really a science, the services of which can make human life more blessed than what it is to-day, not by any magic, but by hastening the evolution of the spirit in wisdom and power. It is the natural consequence of truly spiritual life. It is really the exhibition finally of the power of the spirit and not only of subtle forces.

The full significance and possibilities of the spiritual life cannot even be imagined were one not to follow the whole course of evolution it brings forth in its train. Mankind in its slavery to the habits of life, is not prepared to forego them and re-shape them and to receive the privileges and the changes that an occult life is sure to introduce. Spirituality envisages fundamental changes in our whole nature. The spiritual-force cannot brook resistance and commands an unquestionable obedience and surrender from the total being, for there it can redeem its blessings and privileges. Its masterful impulse cannot take hold of our being, and express its complete nature if the old habits of thought and modes of action still persist. Spirituality first makes the discovery of the central being of man, where his personality appears in its luminous splendour, and then traces out the thread of connexion between it and the divine. So long as the central being is not discovered, there is no possibility of the full fruition of spiritual life. The fundamental connexion must be established in the dynamism of the spirit. Spirituality remains only a surface concern if this is not done at the outset, and it is because of this that the dynamic identification does not take place in our basic nature. Spirituality always remains either as a matter of intellectual intuition, or fine aestheticism or moral intuition. Philosophic or aesthetic contemplation can acquaint us with these fine promises, but they are promises within the bounds of higher intuitive formations. Occultism discovers the dynamism of the spirit which carries with it these fine privileges, but something more in the shape of the release of divine force immanent in our nature. Spirituality, as commonly understood has ignored such formations, and has sought its promise in intellectual or aesthetic transcendence, leaving aside the vaster possibilities of divinising life.

Occultism throws open the inner forces working in us and activates them for a spiritual purpose. The experience of the whole world linked up in the bonds of the spirit, and the whole of life moving in the rhythm and joy of spirit is rare thing. Eventually with it a phase is enterned upon where the manifest details of existence acquire a new meaning in the divine setting. This divine regulations of life is not a matter of inference, but of direct and immediate knowledge. What remains otherwise a distant vision becomes a fact of direct realisation; and in addition to this it throws helpful light on the functioning of the force in every part of our being and directs it in response to the master urges emanating from the central being. Occultism renders a three fold service :—(1) It unearths our hidden being, (2) It reveals a correspondence between the psychic and the cosmic forces, (3) It discovers our central being which regulates the forces in such a way as the slavery to nature may be shaken off, and the divine will and the power be activated in us.

It is naturally associated with spirituality. Spirituality is the indrawn urge to be associated with the divine, occultism is the natural consequence, sought or unsought. It has spontaneous expression with the spiritual aspiration. It emerges when the spirit makes our nature transparent and removes inertia and ignorance.

Philosophic life, which mentally envisages eternal truths may not feel the presence and the power of the occult forces, for here the appraisement of truth does not become dynamic in life. The spirit of truth descends and introduces vast changes in our mental vital being, the expansive force which spiritual realisation releases cannot but affect our whole being. There is an organic connexion between the different strata of being, and if one part is influenced, the others can not remain unaffected. Hence the truth-seers often possess vaster powers, for their being becomes cosmically tuned.

Truth-realisation cannot leave us cold. But its effect becomes tremendous when the force of truth radiates every part of our being and releases the hidden energies of the soul. It is then that a higher vision, revealing the divine constitution of things and beings, attracts and inspires us. It is here that man realises the supra-natural powers and gifts, for his faculties draw inspiration from the divine source.

Philosophy gives wisdom, and sometimes glimpses into divine wisdom. Occultism makes the whole nature divinely activating all the parts of our being. Divine wisdom, divine movement and divine being go together. The complete re-birth is not possible unless there is the invitation and the acceptance of the divine life from every part of our being and its complete saturation with it.

The saturation is not possible if all the organs of our being are not divinely attuned or inspired, if they are not brought under the re-shaping divine through all the grades of being. This release of divine force in every strata of Being is a sure moulding power which vivifies the grossest part of being and spiritually enlivens them. A new illuminating force gets hold of our being and formulates it in a divine way.

Occultism therefore gives a new birth as it were to our being in dynamic spirituality. Its ideal is to spiritualise the total being in all parts and to inmortalise life. It introduces then a superior tone in every part of being and gradually makes it fully divine. Occultism gives this promise to usher in divine being in us in its fullness and intensity and presents the divine man not only in silence, but in its divine stature of being, divine beauty and divine power. It is the foretaste of the hidden possibilities that are hidden in man and released rarely. But it indicates a new line of superior spiritual evolution and seeks to change the being in its appearance by drawing out the deeper force and by activating it. Now we shall see the bearing of this force on the varied expressions of life.

CHAPTER VII

OCCULTISM, ART AND RELIGION

Occultism has its intimate relation to Art and Religion. To art it gives its occult and psychic vision, by which the inward beauty and excellence is envisaged. Occultism releases the creative instinct to its full height. It gives the creative exaltation, and the stream of creation flows, spontaneously and easily, without the least conscious effort. 'A work of art is the unique result of a unique temperament. Its beauty comes from the fact that the another is what he is'. (Oscar Wilde). True, but it makes a great difference when the creative stirring flows from the hidden recesses of being, when one is possessed by the gentle influence of the divine artist active in nature and spirit. This artist has his vision extended to the archetypal shapes and beauties not usually revealed to everybody. The artist here gets into the occult beauties that are in the heart of things and impresses them upon his creations. The occult-artist sees these beauties in the moment of supreme exaltation and the creative forces find their expression through him. He is sensitive to the beauties of the vital order the beauties of the spiritual order with their distinctive differences and the creative expression takes shape according to his inspiration, receptiveness and inner sympathy. The finer details in the composition are better revealed to the occult than to the ordinary vision.

and naturally the occultist is on a vantage ground. He realises better the true individuality of things and beings in which is centred the interest of the artist. This individuality represents the divine essence and expression. The soft lustre, the delicate poses, the vibrative radiations are immediately felt by the occultist by his inner sympathy, and naturally he is privileged as an artist, for art, after all, requires the creative vision. The creative vision extends in the case of the occultist to the very core of existence. The occult knowledge can help the artist to bring out the deeper rhythms and basic harmonies in his creations. The occultist enters into the world of subtle colours, forms and gives expression to the aestheticism that is rare. The direct seeing gives the forceful creative powers.

Occultism does not offer any theory of God. God is living to the occultist. The intellectual theories that interest a philosopher have no serious meaning to the occultist for he draws his inspiration from a height far above the intellect. His vision is not blurred by hazy theories. he has the soft and iridescent light of truth in its silent glory. Here is the supreme revelation which carries with it its conviction and power. Occult consciousness seizes upon the divine in the creative flow of life as well as in its transcendent depths. It reveals the divine nature of things and beings, the divine pulsation of its harmony,and its radiance. The divine is not a far-off reality and its expression not a far-off event. The occultist sees the living God in all the grades of existence. The creative potencies, the psychic forces, are all revealed to him and the divine shaping of things and beings are thus fully understood. The seekers are lifted to a plane of consciousness where nature's crust is removed and the inner sleeping forces are revealed. These forces exhibit the secret functioning of the divine in nature and man, and the real meaning of the immanence of the divine. The divine force does not function in an identical way through the different levels of existence and therefore to the occultist the hierarachy of beings and existence is a potent fact. The hierarchies are real to the occultist, and they exhibit gradations of existence with growing beauties.

The occultist is alive to the distinction of the natural and the super-natural; the spiritual potencies in the natural are patent to him. He does not discard the natural. He is conscious of the forces in the natural order, but he sees clearly the presence of the divine force and its insistent attempt to establish itself completely in it.

This inner seeing makes the occultist an optimist. In the history of events he traces out the divine will and its operation. Naturally the events, however insignificant, have for him an intense meaning and interest. He, it appears, is more interested in the emergence and active expression of the spirit in the order of creation than in its immanence. The occultist refuses to accept the conflict between mind and body. There is the actual attempt of de-materialising matter.

CHAPTER IX.

DE-MATERIALISATION.

In Indian thought mind and body have not been regarded as completely separate and distinct. And therefore, no such theories as Interactionism or Parallelism appear. Mind and body represent two aspects of a single process of change or emergence. They represent different degrees of condensation of the original creative force or Śakti. The inert is apparently inert. It is the sub-dued expression of life and consciousness. At different stages of emergence they appear. The finer can react upon the gross, just as the gross can upon the finer. The relation between the spirit or the self and the emergents in the Tantras is also solved in the same way, for the Tantras do not lend their support to any form of dualism of existence. These emergents are the expressions of the same reality, and mind and body are distincts and not divergents.

The phenomenon of de-materialisation proves the supreme control of mind over body, for it is the mind's capacity of prevailing over matter and of taking subtler shape and form. Matter is plastic and the psychic can take any form. The process of change can be so subtle that it can express itself without the gross form. This of course does not mean that there is no material basis in de-materialisation. It only proves that the psyche can express itself through subtler forms of matter. It is a form of re-incarnation. Re-incarnation does not necessarily mean the complete dissociation of matter from the spirit, for in the evolutionary ascent some form of thin material sheath is necessary for the spirit's expression. It is the psychic vestment.

The psychic is luminous matter energised by spirit directly. It becomes the vehicle of expression of the adepts, through which they can retain their individuality after attaining liberation for cosmic ends and purposes.

De-materialisation is with the occultist not a philosophic insight, but a spiritual promise; and he establishes it by discovering the spirit's urge and formation in matter. Plato has the occult insight when he envisages how the psyche can establish the supreme order and beauty in the prevalent chaos of the material order. The occultist hastens the evolution by making the spiritual force fully active. This blessed privilege is his.

The occultist establishes the harmony of creative life. God to him is creative principle, not the êlan vital of the vitalist. It is *radiant force,* the divine consciring that is active in the heart of things. The religious sense gives direct knowledge of *this force* and acquaints us with its gentle formation, through all things. The supreme fulfilment is reached when the occultist becomes identified with this spiritual force and becomes the instrument of the divine formation. The occultist not only sees, he becomes. The seer is the detached observer, the occultist is the creator. He is identified with the force of spiritual creation.

Not in wise passiveness. but in the radiant impulse of creation the occultist finds his great joy for his is the vocation to re-affirm the spirit in nature, and to establish the spiritual federation on earth by removing all obstacles. This inspiration is his by his special fitness which he acquires by the unearthing of the creative spiritual force and power. The occultist is above all *a builder ;* he builds by activating and integrating the spiritual forces.

In this great task of re-building and establishing the divine order of things, he is helped by the supreme grace and the occult hierarchies; and the occultist is personally conscious that the spiritual connexions are widely established and inextricably mingled. He receives directly, in order that he can profusely give. The occultist more than any body is fully conscious of the community of spirits and his vision extends to the focal point of existence. He draws divine inspiration therefrom. His imagination feels the saturation of the whole existence with the divine spirit, and the supreme influence of the divine in the shaping of things.

This intimate connexion with the focal point of existence endows the occultist with the rare gift, divine vision and divine power. He naturally sees things in their essence and spiritual setting. They are inter-connected in subtle and luminous ways. The forms are radiant, the connexions are rediant and every thing emits beauty, fragrance, life, and joy. They are being constantly charged with lustre, vivacity, force and power by the ready supply from the source. Besides, the animated vision of nature, the occultists feel the direct contact with the exalted presences. They are intermediaries. The novitiate requires their help. They cannot receive directly. The force is softened through the intermediaries. The occult brotherhood* and the hierarchy become a fact of experience, when such help is received. The help is sent mysteriously. None the less it is sent and it is received.

Occult religion then gives the direct consciousness of the radiating centre of peace, light, life and power and this luminous picture of the different grades of things. The vast sense of immensity is his, and he realises it in literal sense. Existence seems at times too overpowering in its majesty, and unless the occult faculties with intensive powers are developed, it becomes difficult to bear the presence of so overwhelming an experience. It is actually measuring the depths of existence, its height and power. The overpowering sense which one feels when one first encounters occult experiences is gradually conquered by the assuring knowledge, which makes his movement free and easy. All existence is surrounded by a halo, a lustre, and is filled up with a spiritual thrill and fervour. None can fully envisage its full possibilities, for this means the complete overshadowing of our human limitations. God alone is the great occultist; the human aspirant can approach the consummation

* The Tantras speak of the *Divya-ougha, Manasougha, Siddha-ougha* Orders. —Vide Lalita Sahasranāma (Verse 37).

according to the fineness of being and constitution. Occultism is a gift of nature; and a special fitness of being is required to fully fathom its mysteries. If the occult sense gives to art its radiant creative impulse, to religion it gives the vividness, and the freshness of life together with wide knowlede, exuberant joy and forceful will.

The religious aspiration produces an inward urge to establish the identification with the dynamic divine. Then the creative urge is invested with a divine force and skill. Art follows religion. The supreme art, which the occultist has the previlege to use and enjoy, is the art of re-making and re-shaping his own being allowing the spiritual force to act upon his entire system, the physical, the vital, and the mental. The spiritual charge takes complete possession of the system, and purifies the mind and makes the body lustrous. The spiritual initiate cannot be missed, his whole form is radiant, and movement graceful. Beauty in the physical being, harmony in the vital-being, and serenity in the mental being are the immediate effect of the religious approach through occultism. This skill in the re-orientation of being is supreme in the occultist, for he knows the secret of modulating, re-forming crude nature. The occultist is the self-builder.

The art of re-making his personality endows him with the secret of influencing others. The wide know ledge of nature, the spontaneous sympathy which it evokes, the direct knowledge of subtle connexions and identities and above all the unity of nature and being enable the occultist to impart a healthy influence. His influence has the sure shaping power upon others. The occultist is the unconscious artist in this sense, the re-maker of man in the true sense of the word.

CHAPTER X.

OCCULTISM AND EVOLUTION.

Occultism speaks of the higher ascents in evolution. To it man is not the measure of all things. Human evolution is still not perfect, for there are forces which do not submit themselves to the spirit completely. The ascent in the scale of evolution suffers. The urge behind the evolution is the spirit, neither energy, nor life, nor mind. The occultist is literally conscious of the truth. This is not mere speculation. It is truth based upon experience. Vitalism, emergent evolution, all begin wrongly. Their approach is crude. It is indeed the claim of occultism. And the proof of this conclusion is sought in the movements of the spirit and their modifying influence upon life and matter. With the disappearance of concentration, of that which appears as matter, life is realised to be fundamentally spirit. Evolution is hastened if the native tendencies of our being are surrendered and the underlying current of the spirit be active in us. Practical occultism constantly pursues the reformation and re-orientation of being by tracing the direct connection with the spirit and by its complete infusion. The greatest attraction of occultism lies in its exercising the transforming power of the spirit. Occultism traces the fine stages of matter, it really dissolves it into force or energey and conceives a luminous form of existence, with a higher potency, and power. Every form of existence has its radiant and shining force, a superb colour and spiritual aura. To the occultist this aura is the index of the spiritual potency of things. Every thing in nature has its aura ; and when the occult rays, sound and forms, are manifested, nature reveals the inner being of things, their subtle and intimate connexion with the spirit, sometimes their spiritual essence.

These superb beauties of things indicate that matter in its high state of attenuation loses its crudities, its stiffness. Evolution then proceeds to the revelation of the ethereal forms of things and beings. In this order the blinding force of matter is completely removed. Not that the basic support of life in matter is completely removed, but the support becomes such that life can express its vivacity, sprightliness much better. The material universe is to the occultist much finer and more beauteous than what is presented before us. The world appears fresh and beautiful, for every thing emits a freshness, fragrance and life.

Occult knowledge is not only intensive, it is extensive too. It refuses the bounds of space and reports happenings at a distance. Clairvoyance, clairaudience are only natural. In the case of the fine occultist the sense and mind become highly sensitive to be able to receive impressions from the higher planes of existence They become fine, powerful and highly receptive to the finer ethereal vibrations. The mind traces the cue to the wider life, and becomes the centre of intuitions which otherwise remain hidden. Wonderfully enough, a new order of imageries with fine creative power reveals itself and the imagination becomes directly stirred under the direct influence of spirit.

Imagination is the faculty that is more intimately connected with the spirit, for it is the faculty of creation; and the spirit getting hold of it becomes the successful author of a new creation and revelation. The imagination and the will are two most important faculties which the occultist exercises in order to build up someth g effective. The will takes the cue from the divin l for effective expression and the imagination supp s the definite form of creative expression. The occultist becomes cognisant of the depth of our mind, the utmost expansion of our faculties with their subtle powers, and the possibilities of fine inspiration from higher sources. Evolution is thus hightened and hastened. Man becomes a superman with a finer power of perception, divine imagination, divine will and power. The occultist is aware that the divine power in its immanence is eternally creative, for he feels that the power of creation descends from above. The spirit of God gets possession of us and makes us creative by infusing the divine will and imagination in us. The occult creation is difficult to follow, for very often spirit is missed unless there is some internal sympathy. It introduces a new order of expression by infusing a new life and new power and by adding a new charm. We have then two principal objects in occultism: the first is to release consciousness from its limitations and restricted movements; the second is to make nature so refined that it can release better powers and make finer formation possible. The second is dependent upon the first, for nature releases her powerful emanations when the light of consciousness is reflected upon her. Finer formation goes with fine knowledge, and it is essential for further evolution that the light of higher consciousness should be reflected on every part of our being. Consciousness quickens life. The whole evolution of our being works upon this principle. Evolution, rightly understood, is the constant urge to assimilate wider being and to absorb more fineness and elasticity. The obstacles of our nature are removed by the sure force of the spirit and when the unconscious part of our being, and still more the conscious movements of life, will be reinforced by the infusion of conscious light, evolution will be at its best. Occultism emphasises these two movements : (1) to be clearly conscious in every part of our being : (2) from which follows a natural corollary,—the release of life force and spirit. Conscious life is intermediate between the sub-conscious and the super-conscious. It is influenced by them. Influences from these sources reach it and constantly reinforce it. The creative formations emerge from the sub-conscious or the supra-conscious urges. The unconscious plays a very important role in occult psychology. Occult psychology traces the presence of consciousness in the physical and the vital mind. Its range extends to still greater heights. Occultism as science affirms the connexion between the sub-conscious and the super-conscious, and as art it reveals the clue to their connexion.

When these extremes meet, the cosmic consciousness is revealed to us. The occultist aspires to this. It gives him the rare and the blessed privilege not only of a wide consciousness but also of a free movement in all planes of existence. The art which gives the occultist such knowledge and power is the art of removing the distance of the sub-conscious by the forces of the superconscious. The occultist has superior advantages, because he is blessed with the secrets of every part of our being, and the thread of connexion that runs through them. The gift is only his; hence the power that he exercises, and the knowledge that he enjoys.

Occultism is the most refined and delicate art of modulating our being in a way conducive to its graceful and beauteous expression. The supra-conscious throws its light and influence upon the sub-conscious and reveals the functioning. The influence can be deep. It establishes a harmony in the conscious life. The supra-conscient forces work in this direction. There is a necessity in it. The higher and wider revelation in the supra-conscious cannot keep pace with it. Nature observes strict economy. The upward ascent in consciousness helps transformation in the lower, otherwise the fine evolution in our consciousness and being cannot advance. There is a thread of connexion between the apex of consciousness and the sub-conscious and the inconscient. A continuous stream of inspiration can pass through this path and can make the lower vehicle luminous in order that consciousness may find clear expression even there. This task lies before the occultist.

This is specially his own. The occultist directly establishes a connexion between the central being and the sub-liminal and the supra-liminal extremes. This is the greatest art of life. This direct connexion makes it convenient for the supra-conscious light to pass into the subconscient and to effect a gradual transformation. It gives regeneration. Nature is brought under the control of the spirit which re-shapes and makes it the medium of transmission

This is done in two ways (1) conscious influence and (2) by unconscious influence. In each case there must be detachment. Nature must be left to herself. Her depths must be stirred. The tidal waves from the unconscious depths sometimes fill us and the creative forces operate, building a new order, a new architecture beyond the finest imagination. Such unconscious creation is set up in dreams and dreams have a great importace in occult psychology.

There are many theories on dreams. The wish fulfilment theory is true in its own way. But it does not go far. It reduces the whole psychic being of a man into desire and instinct and is therefore a partial account of a complex phenomenon. Repression makes the forces go deep in our nature, and finds an outlet for them in sleep. There are vital urges which have in them the power of ideal creation. Vital memory gathers up in unconscious moments and makes a construction of them even in the semi-conscious state. The vital desire makes up vital imagination. It is good so far as it goes. But the psycho-analyst does not see the architecture of the dream which does not indicate wish-fulfilment or things of that type. Sometimes its range of creation, its delicacy, its vividness, its luminosity, its fine aroma, its swift march of delightful construction, the deeper wisdom of the spirit which it revals vouschafe for it a different and still more mysterious explanation and occult formation. Man is a protean being, endowed with diverse forces. He has hidden layers and there is sometimes the inrush into dream-consciousness of forces and formations which are beyond the purview of common experience.

A. E. George Russel tells us "Our brain is full of living creatures as our body is thronged with tinny cells" I know my brain is court where many living creatures throng and I am never alone with it. There are creatures in the soul which eye and speak through them to us in dream, so that we have their voice, and it is with us in our minute microsmic fashion even as it was said of the universe that it is a soliloquy of deity wherein Ain-Soph talks to Ain-soph". The occult psychology speaks of dreams as the formation of psychic forces which are released in the extreme subjectivity of the consciousness. These are visitations of the forces of the super-liminal heights of existence. On rare occasions the soul is elevated to a higher plane of consciousness, or some higher force descends into consciousness. The imageries of such dreams are unique, their creations are unique. Call them the creation of the soul or the visitations of finer beings, they reveal a new order of existance more elastic, more luminous. The soul enjoys a new universe with its soft rhythms and transparent imageries and the inner spirit of things and beings. There is no restriction of space. Sometimes the dream universe becomes vast, in which are crowded radiant beauties, solemn dignities. Their truth may be and is often questioned. Experience is the bar ; experience is the helper.

Life is associated with memory. Memory is the conserving force of life. This conserving force directs the new formations, preserving a continuity. There is memory in our vital life which tells its story, and if the subtle thread of memory can be traced the vital-mind can express successfully its movements, their functioning, their relations to the still sub-stratum of being and their connexion with the higher mental life. Nay, if one is persistent it can reveal the wider cosmic vital-life with which one's vital being is intimately connected and from which occasionally and unconsciously and draws more life and power. Such experiences may often prove obstructions, if we are engrossed in them ; they reveal the laws and the formations of sub-mental life, and unless the thread of finer formations is pursued, the occult exprience is confined.

But life or the spirit-force functions in the superconscient, and there is a connexion between the vital and the supra-conscient formation, for they are graded existences not discontinuous but arranged in a hierarchy with subtle relations which integrate them in a unitary system. And it is possible therefore to pass into the finer world by tracing the luminous thread of connexions. Dream expriences help here. In dreams at times the insurgent forces of the vital nature are held in abeyance, and to the aspiring soul, the finer conscious life reveals its formations. The aspirant is lifted to the planes of existence otherwise inaccessible. These visitations from the higher reaches are in the beginning occasional, and often follow when the aspiring soul becomes free from the solicitations and impressions of waking consciousness. The aspirant finds the key to the subjective consciousness with which the supra-conscious is directly connected. And if the memory of such dream experiences can be retained and revived in waking consciousness, it helps the repetition of such experiences. Memories of such shining experiences are never lost; they become the sure power of transformation. These memories work sometimes very powerfully in the waking consciousness and the representation becomes vivid and living. This conscious functioning of the memory gives better acquaintance with the spirit or life-force.

Once the relations have been established between the conscious and the supra-conscious life it becomes easy to feel the inspiration and to receive this infusion direct. The waking consciousness can forego its usual objective reference, pass at once into a subjectivity and enter into higher reaches. This inception in the waking stage takes place when the habit of conscious detachment has been well established. Consciousness attends here to the objective solicitations as well as to the superior subjective inspirations. It becomes easy, free and spontaneous. It exhibits the grades of our consciousnesss, objective and subjective, cosmic, supra-cosmic, all reacting to the different forces playing in the different universes. The ascent affords a wider and finer consciousness and a knowledge of the higher world. The higher worlds in the scale of ascent reveal newer life, diviner delights; what is more, it exhibits the vital and psychic knots at the different parts of our being, which keep consciousness restricted in its expressions and life confined in its play. The occultist breaks the psychic knots and releases the vital, psychical, spiritual forces. The higher and wider consciousness are related to the vital and psychic centres. The inner connexion becomes so well established that the whole being becomes diffused with the higher spiritual potency, power, and and radiance. Consciousness is immanent in our whole being, but it is not felt equally every-where. The occultist has extensive knowledge of the vital and the psychic as well as the spiritual forces.

Occultism establishes a correspondence between the psychic and the cosmic life. A time comes when the knowledge of this correspondence becomes direct and immediate. Then it becomes possible to draw directly from the cosmic forces, be inspired and moved by them. The same force functions psychically and cosmically, and when its roots have been discovered, it then becomes possible to function from the source, if the consciousness at this height becomes well established. This indeed is the greatest privilege given to the ocult adepts, which can work freely in the higher planes of existence, and inspire world movements by their influence and power. But they cannot disturb the cosmic process, unless they feel the divine urge, for the occultist better than any one else feels the divine working of the order and knows the time and the movement when the divine will becomes active to set in a new order, and the divine influence released for the purpose. The occultist feels the divine impulsion in the creative order and adjusts it accordingly. He is the divine agent in the human order of things, either personally helping the divine forces to take shape or instrumentally emitting inspiring influence through others. Such is the mystery of the occult order. The Tantras accept the tradition of the seven layers of existence, arranged in a hierarchy according to their plasticity and fineness, and trace out a correspondence between these planes of existence and the layers of our consciousness. This law of correspondence between the inner and the outer world is the unique feature of Hindu Cosmology. This law is the basis of the art of life in the Tantras. This art essentially consists in getting hold of fine psychic forces in us and through them to open up hidden layers of our being in order that the direct connexion may be established between the physic and the cosmic forces. Man does not stand separate from the finer cosmic forces, and so long as he can not find out the principle of parallelism that governs the inner and the outer, the knots of our nature confine us to our present dimension of being. When the psychic self is active in us, the truth of correspondence becomes evident. We get intimation of cosmic powers,

CHAPTER XI.

THE GRADES OF CONSCIOUSNESS.

The Tantras speak of the grades of consciousness. The distinction is drawn according to the function of consciousness through the different strata of our complex being. Whatever the metaphysical affirmation may be, the psychological and vital experienences point to the more luminous and the less luminous expressions of consciousness. The modern psychological distinction of the conscious and the unconscious is anicipated in the Tantras and in some respects their analysis is finer, their localisation is more accurate. Not much light has been as yet thrown on the unconscious, (excepting what little has been done by the psycho-analysts) and the relation of the higher psychic or spiritual experiences and the unconscious is still a mystery. The psycho-analyst finds the libido or *élan vital* as the supreme principle and considers all finer development as ramfications of it. The unconscious may be the fundamental structure not disturbed by the fluctuations of a transitory consciousness, but its nature and range still remain a mystery. The unconscious, according to Eastern wisdom, comprises within it the total range of the conscious life, including the individual and collective inherited dispositions and forces—vital, mental, psychical, as well as those which do not come within the ordinary reach of consciousness, viz, the super-conscious, and the cosmic-conscious. They also represent the conscious life in its functioning, far beyond the sub-conscious and the conscious, which opens out vaster and subtler harmony. There is the subtle connexion between the higher reaches and the psychic and vital life but the line of connexion is felt by those who can readily follow the stretches of consciousness extending far beyond vital and mental life having only remote connexion with our individual and collective vital and mental make-up, generally called personality.

Consciousness is all-prevading and immanent everywhere. We can speak of the physical consciousness, the vital-mental consciouness. These are true of our normal experience. They become facts of clear experience when the consciousness in these parts develops. Then the parts and their functioning become clearly reflected in consciousness. These parts become as it were illuminated. The sensitive can directly see their functioning. Affections from the different parts are communicated to the brain, the occultist locates the feeling in the parts affected.

There runs the luminous-thread of connexion between the different layers of conscious life, and when the entire thread is directly felt, the whole existence in its occult nature is revealed vertically and horizontally. The occultist with his rare insight can see the functioning of the forces in all planes of existence, and can feel the unique individuality of man. Each individual has a distinct nature. The occultist is aware of this, he can realise the scale of evolution reached by individuals. This is a very important truth which is often ignored, for the ordinary psychology does not proceed far enough to see the finer forces and perfection or the hidden depths of man's nature. The occult psychology and physiology are in eresting on this account.

The study of the localisation of conscious and vital functioning has to the occultist absorbing interest and the occultist carries the process of localisation to perfection. He unearths the psychic centres in all parts of our being and connects directly the functioning of the different parts of the system with them. But it is not the general vital, physiological or psychological functioning that interests the occultist. He is engrossed with the functioning of the spirit in and through them.

Naturally the occultist discovers something unique of which the physiologist, the vitalist and the psychologist are not aware. Fine shades of colour, gentle ripples of delightful harmonies, fill our being. The study of the layers of our being is interesting, in as much as it enables us to see the result of the spiritual infusion in its different parts. This indeed is the theme of practical occultism. Man, inspite of the many outer coverings of his being, has a *central being* which connects him with the periphery as well as the centre of cosmic consciousness. The central being receives the spiritual sap from the source : and this reception becomes continuous when the conexion of the central being with the cosmic consciousness is well established. Then a kind of spiritual charge fills our whole being. It removes the inertia, the old habits and the clingings of our being, and reveals the inner working of our physical, vital, and mental nature and even their correspondence with the cosmic vital, cosmic mental and cosmic physical. Following the law of correspondence the occultist in moments of deep absorption can see and feel their subtle functioning anywhere. Nature stands revealed in her operation. This knowledge is essentially knowledge by *identity* made possible by discovering the affinity of our being with every thing. Indeed occultism and practical training in it are inviting because of the kind of knowledge and sympathy it affords. It goes far to heal up the deficient constitution by making the finer forces function in us. Nature fills up the deficiencies, if she can be properly modulated by waking up the underlying consciousness of the deficient parts. There is no magic in occult science, excepting that it tunes up our being to a high pitch to activate our consciousness fully. The service that occultism does is the reaffirmation of consciousness throughout our being which releases the fine forces of nature and converts it gradually into a fit vehicle of the spirit. The physical, the vital, and the mental all harmoniously react to the spiritual expression and a deeper harmony is established in them. The occultist, enjoys the divine harmony everywhere in him a well as outside of him. Harmony fills life, harmony is life. This harmony follows the grades of consciousness. The higher the reach, the deeper the harmony, the greater the range of being. When the higher pitch in life and consciousness has been a matter of direct experience, its harmony can descend downwards in the lower parts of being, establishing their order and unison. This indeed is the great art of removing the contradictions of nature and establishing the identical tune everywhere. The vibrations of spirit make it possible when they are firmly established in every part of our composite being. The occultist can work in all the grades of consciousness and is aware of their inter-connexion.

CHAPTER XII

EVOLUTION OF YOGA.

The Tantras give the most extensive reading of the Yoga. They show the development of Yoga in many phases. The traces of Yoga, especially in its essential feature, can be found in the Upaniṣads. Its systematic study and practical application are found in Patañjali, who gives it the form of a scientific system of thought and discipline. In the Upaniṣadic texts the psychology of the Yoga and its practical discipline occur. Sometimes indications are given, and not detailed teaching and detailed practices. But the general indications suffice to give perfect guidance. The Upaniṣads differentiate the soul from its sheaths, the higher mind, the mental, the vital and the physical being, and emphasise the discriminating consciousness that can truly separate appearance from reality. The Upaniṣads advise concentration on the forces composing our being, including our physical, vital mental, higher mental, bliss-ful-self. This gives the perfect knowledge of the interior being of man. The sheaths, with which the self seems to be indentified, are felt more as instruments of expressions of the self than as the self. This differentiating consciousness discovers the self as the transcendent consciousness. It is neither the subject, nor the instrument of its expression.

It is the path of wisdom in the Upaniṣads. There is the path of power, in which the instrumental faculties get intensive in strength and power by finer developement of being. Power is natural concomitant to wisdom. It emerges from the subtle movement of being. In some of the Upanishads, e,.g,. Chandoyga, Nada Vindu, the accounts of spiritual powers are given ; and they are of various kinds. They follow the spiritual potency that is generated in us, because of the finer oscillations of our being. It is the inevitable consequence of the supreme choice and its fulfilment. But power is the least thing sought. Wisdom is not power. The Upanishads have not laid any stress upon it, though they have seen its inevitableness. The Yoga in the Upanishads is the Yoga of Knowledge, the path of supreme knowing, the path of vidya (light) and the supreme fulfilment. To the wise men nothing can remain hidden. He has the supreme revelation of Truth. The wise man is never fascinated by power knowing fully well that truth is higher than power. The path of power is prescribed for the aspirant, not for wisdom. The path of power endows us with subtler harmonies which allow spiritual privileges and subtler delights, and sometimes subtle gratification. These powers really confine us sometimes to solicitations and gratifications of vital being, and sometimes to the delightful harmonies of widening consciousness. The aspirant must be prepared to forgo these privileges of esotoric powers to reach Truth. Some of the Upanisads speak of the subtle shining passage of the Susumna passing through the central nervous system upto the brain and finally opening out into cosmic consciousness. The secret of this approach is given here, but its development is seen in the Tantras.

The spiritual consummation as laid down in the Upaniṣads inspires the spirituality of the future ages Buddhism specially records the psychic revelations and the psychic powers that follow as a consequence to sincere seeking, but which as a rule it admonishes to take no notice of, for they bind the aspirant to power.

In Patañjali the Yoga has been essentially the Yoga of Knowledge. It gives systematic treatment of the subject. The psychology is improved in as much as it lays down particular methods of concentration on the particular centres, giving us knowledge and power. The Patañjalic Yoga recognises two or three principal psychic centres. It gives a fine ethical code, the art of meditation, the supreme detachment for the realisation of the supreme truth. The art of Yoga finds its clear development, in the account of various forms of Samādhi, giving us the graded knowledge of the creative and the transcendent self. A discrimination between the transcendent self and the creative principle is the sure way to the redeeming wisdom. This is possible at the end of a life of seeking and discipline, and at every stage of the progressive ascent, the seekers are introduced to the truths of the different planes of existence. The knowledge it gives is definite and exact. It gives the rare knowledge of the basic elements of nature, and shows that the physical, the vital and the mental life represent the definite stages in evolution.

The Yoga devlops rare insight which gives the

knowledge of the details of existence. Its method is *intensive penetration* into the layers of existence. It gives analytical knowledge because attention is focussed on the different parts of existence. It gathers up the knowledge of the gross and the fine and the causal and finally of the transcendent. It intuits and reveals in complete detachment to the object. This is true also when the psychic principles are intuited. The psychic or material formations belong to the same category of existence ; the one is fine, the other is gross. The one can reflect directly the light of the soul, the other can hardly reflect it. But their nature does not change thereby.

It will be realised now that the path of knowledge and the path of power are different. Knowledge throws light on reality and makes us free from the cob-webs of an intricate existence.

The path of power endows us with the specific capacities that emanate from the knowledge of the subtle forces functioning either in us or outside us. It is also associated with knowledge of subtler existence, but not with the transcendent wisdom. Power is the natural consequence of access into the finer aspect of the forces functioning in existence. It is attractive, because it increases our vital, mental and psychic capacities. It gives occult knowledge. It gives occult powers. Patañjali does not favour this acquisition of powers. They are charms which bind the soul to the delights of subtler experiences and subtler movements. They are traps to prevent the march to freedom. Patañjali gives an extensive account of the powers that follow in the path, but everywhere power is associated with knowledge.

Power denies us the joy of aloneness, Kaivalya. The Tantric Yoga is very vast in its scope, it includes both the paths. It does not denounce power. Rather it welcomes it. It gives the freedom of knowledge, and the spontaneity of power. Knowledge gives the transcendent freedom, power, the freedom over life and its movements. The Tantras never lose sight of the dynamism of spirit and never underestimate the creative power of will. The world is will and will is power.

Practically the Tantras envisage all kinds of spiritual evolution which proceed from the growth of the inner spirit and force. The ideal of the supreme existence as endowed with extraordinary powers and supreme spiritual skilfulness moving in consonance with the cosmic will is the concrete ideal in the Tantras. This is indeed the path of power, but power not to bind the soul, rather to fulfil the hidden potentialities and finally to achieve the transcendent bliss. The Tantras exhibit the divine powers that man possesses, and therefore, without totally rejecting them, revives them in our life so that they may be helpful and not a bar. Power is the helper.

This is the special feature of the spirituality in the Tantras laying down a course of evolution and ascent which allows satisfaction to all parts of our being, at the same time providing a spiritual momentum which surely carries us to the goal. Power demonstrates the efficacy of the Tantric discipline by redeeming occult knowledge and infusing occult inspiration. The minimum realisation is indicated by its intensity. Knowledge and power are associated in this way till the final goal is reached in wisdom. This has been the secret of the hold of the Tantras. Deficiencies in nature are healed up and man evolves into a super-man.

This ideal of super-man has a great fascination. It is no abstract idea. It is purely concrete. Man is elevated into a scale of being when he is man and still something more. The super-man exhibits a new scale in evolution when knowledge is intuitive, delight serene, feeling embracive and will cosmic.

This concrete dynamic ideal is emphasised, because the Tantras accept the ideal of power along with the ideal of freedom. The freedom they invite is the freedom of silence along with the creative freedom of spirit. They see the highest beatitudes in the transcendent existence. They do not ignore the psychic development which follows the ardent spiritual aspiration, for the path of the Tantras is essentially the path of life and they cannot be quite insensitive to life's finer expressions and development. Because of this combination of life's harmony with Silence, the Tantras have been the source of intensive attraction. The art of the Tantras lies here. It discovers all the secret forces of our nature and their rhythmic modulations. The psychic resonance of being, revealing the freshness and plasticity of life with its flashes of ethereal beauty and the harmony of cosmic dignity opens out the wider vistas of existence. Beauty, power, and symmetry go along with this. The adept sees revealed before him the transcendent Holiness, with superb dignity and majesty. The super-man enjoys the supreme peace, as well as the swift flow and movement of life and spirit. This enviable realisation is his, because of the psychic unfolding of his being. The super-man reaches a new stage in the scale of evolution, where the individual will is identified with the cosmic will and the individual loses its past history and gets a re-orientation. There may be different types of super-man. Some may excel in knowledge, some in power, some in love and compassion, some may also be endowed with a completer identification and may exhibit beauty as well as majesty, compassion as well as power, trancendent knowledge as well as cosmic movement. Such possibility is reached when the identification with the cosmic will reflects the world-proces in a different way and with a different idea of values. The super-man overcomes completely the human ways and reflects truth and values in a cosmic sense. The truth will be the utmost extension of being, and the truth of a particular thing will be measured by its capacity of reflecting the absolute existence by the amount of identification with it. The degrees of Truth will be a natural conclusion, both from the theoretic and pragmatic view point. Theoretically truth is being, the capacity of being determines the truth of a particular existence, pragmatically the power of radiating its force over a small or large compass will determine its truth. Truth has an expansive force. This power of expansion is really the power of radiating its force and influence. And this essentially determines its values.

What is more, the super-man is in wake of the cosmic and the supra-cosmic existence because of his psychic receptivity. The barrier which divides one from the cosmic correspondence is removed, and the super-man is put in direct communication with the heights of existence. He becames conversant with its laws and expressions which, naturally, he sees and knows better. His insight goes into the heart of things. He follows the string of the cosmic life and follows the cosmic powers,–a new order with the root-power and the graces that go along with it. Every psychic centre of his being vibrates with divine influence and corresponding to the different centres. A new vista in realisation opens.

This concrete ideal the Tantras present before us for they want us to enjoy the different scales of harmony in the wider life, so that the whole of existence can be fathomed in its depth, extensity and height. The super man should be aware of life's expression in all the different planes of existence. Here lies the practical importance of the Tantras; even in actual life it gives us a freedom from the restricted ways and ideas of life and acquaints us with fine forces beyond the possibilities, beyond the ken of ordinary sight. The spiritual fecundity, providing divine joy and power along with the Calm, is the chief attraction.

To identify Tantricism with vitalism would be to commit a mistake. True, the Tantric discipline intensifies our dynamic nature. The Tantras do not lend their support to vitalism as ordinarily understood. Since the whole being gets a start the vital nature also gets a quickening and rejuvenation, but that does not support the usual opinion that Tantricism is a crude form of vitalism. It is the least part of it. The Tantras expressly accept the cosmic principle of will and not of life and therefore they cannot urge upon the vital expression and the vital joys. A vital re-inforcement may follow the spiritual and the psychic opening; but the harmony that is generated together with the vital awakening keeps us from harm's way. The delicate sensation together with the vital harmony establishes a peace in our vital and physical being; and they shake off their inherent inertia and restiveness and enjoy the calm and the harmony that descend upon them. The tantras never maintain the evolution of mind and spirit from life, though they always establish a harmony between the vital and the spiritual nature.

The powers emerge from the different parts of our being, from the expansion of the vital or the mental self or from the still higher parts of our being. All powers are not helpful. They are positively injurious, unless the powers harmonize with the spirit. The Tantras, therefore,condemn the vital powers, as not helpful to Enlightenment.

But there are powers, specially those that proceed from the higher self that become really helpful. The soft lusture shed from the centre of our being, the will that is irresistible, and the love that redeems, become then living facts before us. Their wide amplitude and cosmic character fascinate and inspire us. The powers that emerge from the spirit are sure indications of our evolution and progress. They secure confidence in the path, and uitimately resore the belief in the victory of the spirit. These powers embrace cosmic dimensions. This is a rare possibility but it is there. The Tantras conceive a spiritual hierarchy of adepts of different degrees of powers and knowledge.

Such adepts have direct ingress of psychic light that indicates lines of development and growth. Science speaks of the cosmic rays. In the light of this discovery it is not difficult to understand the existence and the nature of the psychic light and spirit-rays. Professor Millikan says, 'These rays (cosmic) come from beyond the Milky way and also' that there is in the universe much more energy in the form of cosmic rays than in the form of heat and light'. He continues 'there are a few of the cosmic rays that have energies as high as ten billion of electron-Volts, so that these fall into the range to be expected from the sudden and complete transformation of the whole mass of some of the lighter atoms into radiant energy'. This discovery is of immense help to understand the spirit-ray of the occultist. The occultist speaks of the psychic rays revealing the depth of our inner being and the grades of subtler existences and the hierarchies of being. The psychic light is intensely lumious, and highly vibrative. It has an intense penetrative power. It penetrates into all the levels of existence, the physical and the vital, and into still great depths. It rejuvenates it by infusing currents of light and the stream of life. The path to power and enlightemment is here, for it reflects the psychic light and its direct connexion with the divine light and will. The full height of evolution on this path cannot be conceived by the intellect. The subjective mind can receive its flashes.

Those who walk in the path of powers are endowed with a superior consciousness and becomes gradually acquainted with the working of the universal forces and get identified with them. Knowledge first, then power. The path of power is delicate, though it introduces us to the richness of spiritual and occult life. It is never given to those, who are not completely selfless. It is better to be cut of it than to be in it for selfish purpose.

CHAPTER XIII.

VALUE IN THE TANTRAS.

Every higher reach in being is associated with a reach in higher value, in the sense of freedom from the limitation of being and power. The will escapes from its finititude and attains an identification with the cosmic will. Personality is not lost, but it attains higher intensity and force and our intuition and movement become cosmic. To feel and to be identified with the cosmic urges really opens a new compass in our being and knowledge and attains the spiritual values of things and beings. To understand and properly measure the spiritual dynamism immanent in things and beings will be the estimation of their values and the measurement of their being. The Tantras measure value by its spiritual effectiveness and spiritual power. The idea of value is associated with will. When the will moves in consonance with the world of wills, the highest value is reached. Conservation of values is the fundamental axiom of religion. The realm of ends or the kingdom of spirits has been set forth as the spiritual objective. The Tantras go further. A perfect unison with the universal or cosmic spirit is a precursor to a further end, viz.. identification of the human and the divine will. And this identification shapes our will according to the cosmic will and allows us to assimilate the divine nature within us.

The world of values acquaints us with the free movement of spirits, their power and capacity of reflecting the harmony of the kingdom of spirits. When our being is saturated with the force of the spirit, the identification of will takes place. In the spiritual order intensive harmony occasionally establishes this identification and a new possibility arises viz., the infusion of cosmic force and power. This is a rare possibility. Such identification introduces a new conception in spirituality,– the diffusion of the divine force through a particular centre in order that the spiritual order of things may be established. The Tantras establish a direct connexion with the realm of the spirit, and in the course of history, the infusion of the divine force and power becomes necessary in order that the spirit may have a direct ingress in the world order. It makes possible the gradual unfolding of the mind, a new sense develops in man and makes evolution in spirituality possible.

The idea of liberation which the Tantras along with the Vedanta Philosphy indicate, goes beyond the ordinary ideas of value ; for here either the will is completely transcended, or over-shadowed by the cosmic will. The finite will is a limitation. This limitation is to be overcome by the installation of the cosmic will in us. So long as the personal will persists, complete harmony is a rare possibility. Spirituality is the removal of the personal will and the infusion of the supreme will. It is a growth in the art of seeing our effectiveness.

The Tantras along with the Vedanta maintain that

in spiritual life the dynamic identification is indeed what allows freedom from the restricted sense of personality. This identification elevates us to its more exalted being wholly possessed by the spirit.

This invests us with the supreme felicity of existence and freedom of movement and acquaints us with the unbounded harmonies and modulations of the divine life, with the divine powers in their cosmic regulations, spiritual stirrings and expressions beyond the cosmic life. Such liberated souls are the transmitters of spiritual force and powers; they are Man-gods on earth to work out the divine plan or to give it a right shape through cosmic history. Such divine personalities usher in new epochs of civilisation, and though they are entirely one with divine life, they are not immediately cut off from this life on earth. They become an instrument to the emergence of a spiritual expression in civilisation. Such souls are really the intermediaries between the created order and the divine power.

The Tantras conceive different types of liberated souls according to their degrees of assimilation and inspiration. There will be naturally a hierarchy according as the inspiration is direct and continuous. The finest type is the continuous possession of the divine spirit and the undivided and integral sense of identification.

The dynamic identification is true of the creative spirit. It can go far. It can reach the spirit beyond its creativeness, in its a-conceptual priority. This is possible when the supreme poise in being is attained, with the recoiling of the creative spirit. It is the supreme puissance, the Parama Śiva, in its transcendent aloneness. "When the essence of one's being as the Supreme Puissance emerges, one attains the supreme bonitus." (Paraśurāma Kalpa Sutraṃ) (1, 6). When the creative energy is withdrawn the supreme puissance has its expressions beyond the world of concrete functioning. It appears as a state of equilibrium and evenness. Parā-Śakti is co-eternal with Śiva.

The supreme value lies there in the freedom from the influence of the five *Kanchukas*. The *Kanchukas* are the limiting forces. They are Kalā, Avidyā, Rāga, Kāla, and Niyati. *Avidyā* restricts knowledge, Kalā restores partly its obscured activity. Rāga is attachment. Kalā brings limited power of action to a subject. It is quite distinct from the function of obscuration which is Avidya. It should be noted here that obscuration cannot be complete. There is limited action and limited knowledge always. Obscuration is partial.

Niyati :— It is the force that determines the character and potency of things. It is because of this that fire burns. It is the formative power.

Avidya obscures the true nature of the self, possessed of *cit, ananda, icchā, jñāna, Kriyā* and the identification of our being with the Parama Śiva.

Kalā represents the order of expression of the psychic mental feelings or states. Niyati determines the casual efficiency of everything. (Mahartha Manjari, Triventdrum Sanskrit Series Page 50). The spirit is unfettered existence and the spiritual seeking consists not in the transvaluation of values, superseding the confined expressions and in embracing consciousness in its commonalty spread. The highest value is therefore a release from mental scaffolding. The finest realisation emerges when consciousness is freed from the personal holding. The dynamic identification at this stage becomes an impersonal being along with the Super-personal transcendence. Progressive spirituality is limited to the realisation of the spirit in its ascending fineness in the different layers and heights of subtler existence. It is inviting in the extreme. It exhibits personality in its finest and subtlest movements. It excels the finest mental development. Mind can not keep pace with it. It naturally oversteps the conception of mental valuations and creative ideals. If the progress is continuously kept up, these heights of new personal beatitudes with cosmic feelings which they inspire are also overshadowed in the super-personal silence of being.

Naturally, the bent of progressive spirituality is to feel the force of wide expansion and a deep urge even to transcend it. The emergence in spirituality is indicated not only in establishing a spiritual order and felloship which are the natural consequence of so ardent and high an aspration but in appraising and identifying with the cosmic plans in order that our spiritual being may fill the cosmic oscillations and finally pass into the Supra-cosmic. Values in the human sense have a secondary place in the Tantras. The human consciousness can so tune itself as to receive directly and feel the heart beatings of the cosmic and supra-cosmic existence.

CHAPTER XIV

THE SUN-LIT PATH.

Here the Tantras exhibit their consummate skill. The spiritual discipline in the Sāmkhya and the Vedanta has been the path of discrimination in the process of extreme withdrawal. The path is essentially the path of Sāmkhya or Jnāna.

The psychological discipline of the Tantras is different. It unfolds the concrete being of man in its diffenent sheaths, and traces out the immanent consciousness. The unfolding of sheaths acquaints us with the forces working in us. But its usefulness lies in exhibiting and almost demonstrating the composition of our being and ultimately discovering the spirit in its formative force and transcendence. The spiritual art is here direct, i.e. not to proceed by a philosophical prepossession but by a direct psychological intuition, by probing deep into the mysteries of our being. This way it has been possible for the Tantras to unearth the physical, the bio-physical, the vital-mental, the mental-psychical, psychical and the spiritual forces of ous being.

The spiritual pursuit, then, throws open to us absorbing fields in the various strata of our being..... each revealing the subtle forces and formations contained there. Unless we become acquainted with these forces, which have cosmic correspondence, we can not sufficiently evisage subtle layers of existence within and without us. The art of the Tantras has been essentially to know the higher range of the spirit and to modulate our being in a way that can give the blessed riddance from the animal-vital impulses, and may vibrate the basic urge of the spirit. This becomes possible when the psychic being is reached.

The Tantras discover a subtle path which establishes a direct connexion between the psyche and the supreme spirit, force and life. The ingress from the central source can filtrate into our whole being through this path. This is called the *Suṣumṇā*.

In the tradition of Indian Yoga, three subtle passages are spoken of, viz. *Iḍā, Piṅgalā and Suṣumṇā.* Ida is connected with the nasal passage on the left, the Pingala is connected with the right. They can be felt under pressure of inhalation and exhalation. Tradition says that Ida is active when the inhalation or exhalation gets clearer inlet or outlet through the left, the Pingala is active when the inhalation or exhalation gets easier passage through the right nostril. Nothing corresponding to them can be shown in modern physiology excepting some subtle functioning in the sympathetic nervous system. These passages are not so important, as the third one Susumna.

It is a commonplace in spiritual science that there are certain centres which are especially sensitive to spiritual influence. There is a spiritual space (better psychic space) according to the Chandogya Upaṇiṣada at the heart centre in which direct influence from the spirit can be felt. The Tantras discover many centres, the most important are supposed to be six. They have become almost classic in Hindu Occultism. These centres control our physical, vital and mental system, but their importance is not so high as the centres of spiritual force. These centres are regarded as psycho-physical, for the psychic changes are accompanied by the corresponding physical movements or actions. Naturally these centres are supposed to be located in certain parts of our being. In reality the spiritual infusion acts upon the vital-physical system. It grows more sensitive, and becomes more vibrative and luminous. Its coarseness is eliminated and it becomes the transmitter of spiritual and psychic force. The Tantras teach the theory of psychic and spiritual transformation. The presence of an intensive force is felt in these centres, and gentle delightful currents are felt there. With these vibrations, the rigidities are removed from our mental, vital and physical system. The centres are, therefore, communicators of the spiritual force to the different parts of our being. They are all connected with one another by a subtle luminous thread. When one becomes active, its force diffuses and spreads over the others. The centres function just like the automatic sympathetic system. This localisation is not to be taken in too literal a sense. This sun-lit path once discerned cannot again go into obscurity and it leads on to the centre of light and spirituality.

The *Suṣumṇā* is really a subtle luminous path that opens into the vaster spiritual space at the top of the brain and connects us directly with the cosmic depths of existence. It really liberates us, in as much as it throws open the flood gate of spiritual energy and makes our vision more and more extended, both vertically and horizontally. By pursuing it we can pass easily out of the body i.e., our consciousness becomes free from its limitations and apparent identification with the body. It is really the path that connects our psychic life with the cosmic life. If one pursues the subtle path of the *suṣumṇā,* one can pass into the expanding consciousness in which the fine equilibrium of our being is established and the vital impulse becomes quiet. The psychic and spiritual energy flows through the *Suṣumṇā.*

It is not active in all men. It does not ordinarily function. It functions only when the utmost stillness is established in our being and when there is a happy poise in it. Our being must be free from all inertia, all uneasiness, all restlessness. Its functioning means the slowing down and practically stopping of the normal habits of thought and action. It holds the key to the psychic opening, and the different layers of the psychic existence.

Wonderfully this psychic opening exhibits the different knots of our being in our physical self, our vital self, our mental and higher mental self. When these knots are released, our consciousness attains freedom from the insistent urges of these centres and their forces. An adept knows these secrets and is free because he can immediately feel his transcendence and mastery over these forces. The occult science gives real freedom by dissociating our consciousness from the life impulse and the forces. It enables us to establish harmony in them and to husband the forces to bring out the fullest development of our personality.

These knots represent the important centres of our being. They have no uniform character and function. Each individual according to his evolution has a psychic individuality according to the centres that function chiefly in him. All centres do not equally function in all men. In some the vital is dominant, in some the mental, or the higher mental. This determines their individuality, character, and even their out-look on life. The psychiatrist is aware of the *infinite shades* of our being, and its different forms and types. The division of the extrovert and the introvert is a general classification. There are mixed types. Even there are varieties of introverts and extroverts. Again the identical force which makes us introverts makes us extroverts, e.g. spiritual introverts and extroverts. Sometimes the inner impelling is followed by the excess of outward discharge. The equilibrium restores the energy which discovers an efficient out-let. A vital type may be both introvert and extrovert. In psychic life the two processes of inwardness and outwardness go together: the normal law of life is the alternation of contemplation and activity.

To the psychiatrist our personality is an interesting study. He sees directly its composition and the invisible forces that are active in us. When the psychic centres function, our personality assumes a greater dignity. The shape and the formation which the personality takes, depend upon the kind of forces that are stirred. The stirring of the centres reinforces knowledge, and spirituality. What is important is to discover the central tendency and the inner sympathy of our being, *to discover its gravity.*

Besides the attraction to our central being, which gives the uniqueness of our individuality, each distinct individual exhibits unusual inclinations, to love, or to power, to wisdom, or to beauty. Every man has a secret pull. This determines his nature and being. This pull indicates his sympathy. his likings and attractions. It gives a formation to his character. It is important to know this. Two broad types may be indicated (1) the vital and (2) the spiritual. The Intellect takes its formations according to its service, either to the life-impulse or to the spirit-force. The other urges of life, aesthetic, moral, axiological, and intuitive can be distributed under the two broad divisions, in accordance with the character of the life-impulse. It may be that the life impulse is dominated by the spirit. The vital expressions take on a spiritual character. The inner life-forces are inextricably related to one another; it is difficult to separate them completely; they blend spontaneously. The division follows the nature of the life-impulse.

In the terminology of mystical science, it is customary to indicate the gradations of our being, as vital being, the psychic being, the spiritual being. The vital being is the exterior self, the psychic being is the interior self. It connects with the spiritual being. It is necessary to discover and to concentrate on the spiritual being in order that the spiritual unfolding may be possible. The usual and the normal bent of our being is to be gradually transferred to our spiritual self. It will give us freedom from the intricate mazes of life, and control the forces by the light of the spirit. The centre of gravitation is to be established in the spirit, in order that the higher centre of consciousness may be established. The spiritual art of the Tantras is the discovery of the luminous self and assimilation of it in our total self. It introduces us to the still higher stretches of the cosmic and the transcendent consciousness.

Whatever may be the natural inclinations or natural sympathies due to the long standing habits of thoughts and actions, they are to be left aside, and the spiritual urge is to be discriminated from the vital or the mental urge. When it is done, the path is easy. The urge of the spirit is active everywhere. And, therefore, it is not impossible to instil inspiration into vital being and eliminate its ignorance, and inertia, and to bring it into harmony with our higher nature. It is somewhat difficult in the case of the vital types, whose higher nature is not well-developed. With the spiritual inspiration the extroverts become spiritually active. A blind impulse cannot give the true lead.

The introverts have natural advantage over the extroverts. They have their being indrawn. Naturally they are given to thinking and contemplation. Our nature is so complex that it will not be safe to call a type exclusively introvert or exclusively extrovert for their characterisation depends upon the functioning of the actual forces. An extrovert may be introvert; an introvert may also be extrovert. In our psychical life, nothing is fixed. Much depends upon the working of the inner and the outer forces.

The forces are generelly active in us. In occult literature, they are called animus and anima. The animus represents the heaven-drawn forces, and anima, the earth-drawn forces. In the composition of our being both these forces are active, but not every-where with the same intensity, the negative force anima is mostly active in vital types.

When the anima is active in us, consciousness projects itself for the most part outwardly. The positive force-animus is active in types which have higher aspirations. These are finer types which are spiritually active.

The spiritual force takes long to be active. The higher centres are activated by the animus. The spiritual force can easily be active there. But the full spiritual developement is possible when all the centres become activated by the force that is generated in contemplation. The Tantras, therefore, take the boldest course to develop the full intensity of consciouness in psychic centres and to establish a correspondence between them and the wider reaches of being. The definite object is to free consciousness from its ego-centric impulsion and to release its cosmic play. The psychic centres, when they are activated, give knowledge along with power. When the fascination of power is got over, wisdom is attained. The self dedicated to wisdom does not exercise power. Power however subtle implies limitations.

The psychic realisation exhibits rhythm in our being which acquaints us with wider stretches of subtle existence. It sheds light on the concealed nature of things especially it gives the first-hand knowledge of the working of the spirit. When the psychic self becomes active the mind and the intellect become more luminous. The psychic self can act independently of the sense-mind, when it is sufficiently developed and report the stretches of existence which can not be otherwise revealed. Sensitive souls can record and feel them.

Psychic knowledge is a form of intution. There are intuitions of our sense and vital life, there are intuitions of the higher mind (of the ideal order). The vital intuitions proceed from the vital feelings, and vital truths. They give us knowledge of the vital order.

The higher mind works somewhat independently of the ratiocinative mind and presents the synthetic view of reality, more of the form than the heart of the reality. It is the vision of the totality and symmetry of existence. Psychic intuition enters into the heart of things and discovers the spirit that takes formation through them. Psychic intuition introduces a new order of realisation and exhibits the divine order and essence of things. A wide sympathy bassed on unfettered wisdom is the immediate fruition. The whole of our existence acquires a new meaning, a new valuation, far superior to what the mind can aspire. It makes psychic intuition a imperative for the spiritual aspirant. It is directly entering into the forbidden horizon, forbidden because it is difficult to enter there with our mental formations and valuations.

The range of psychic intuition is wide. With the emergence of the psychic, a new formation takes place in all parts of our being. Our senses become quickened, giving us distant vision, distant hearing. Our vital life becomes free from obscurities. The mind becomes clarified and luminous ; but these are small promises before the wider revelations of the cosmic consciousness.

The Psychic can be separated from the body and can reflect vibrations from a distance. It is the still-unborn-self pressing for emergence. The possibility of a new evolution lies in this way. When the psychic fully emerges it can be instrumental to a new way of reception and a new source of fruition and power. Nature releases a higher scale of evolution. It removes the vital and the mental limitations and is filled up with delightful freshness and ease. The psychic opening, however desirable, is only the beginning of the still higher consummation in cosmic consciousness, where the knowledge of the whole existence is reflected. It sounds like a myth that evolution can proceed so far as to go beyond the dimensions of space and time and be cosmic in the full import of the term. This promise awaits the liberation of the psychic self. This is still distant, because the psychic self. This is still distant, because the rhythm of life is not established to a degree which can secure this release. When the psychic force presses itself up, and releases the brain, from its normal activities, the impressions of cosmic consciousness, reach us. We transcend the human ways of thinking and living. The desideratum is to assimilate the cosmic consciousness more and more into our being by throwing out the old habits of thought and life.

The psychic has transforming power. When it affects the sensuous being, it gives beauty, when affects the vital being, it gives power, when it affects the mind it gives wisdom. Psychic functioning heightens the stature of our personality by developing its power and magnitude. Our being moves with the measured beats of wider harmony. We are possessed of a divine tremour, with its force. grace and lustre. It blossoms into the divine nature of personality.

The emergence of the psychic is noticed in its initial stages by the direct insight into the heart of beings and things. It removes the barrier and makes the knowledge direct and penetrating. The capacity gradually increases. Before it the nature of things stands disclosed. Their setting in the divine is envisaged. It presents before us what is hidden in nature and man, and becomes the source of the infusion of the divine into us. This is greatly helped by the process of ascent through the graded experience, as indicated by the psychic centres, and subsequently by the forces of descent from the over-mental regions to the sub-conscient mind.

Psychic knowledge has its concreteness too. In a sense it is more concrete. It gives the complete texture as well as the details of being. Its greatest fruitfulness lies in working out a living correspondence between the forces and the outer cosmic powers. It presents a living synthesis in place of a conceptual one. Naturally it extends beyond philosophic knowledge and mental construction.

The psycho-synthesis is naturally an advance upon the mental synthesis. The psycho-synthesis is the new knowledge that the Trantras afford us by overstepping the vital-mental experience. Its potency is immense. The psycho-synthesis extends beyond the psychic and the cosmic correspondence to still higher knowledge in transcendence. This is a rare consummation which is reached when we get to the root of existence.

It thus appears that there is a continuous thread of psychic connexion between all the strata of our existence. If the luminous insight into all the strata can be attained the whole existence stands revealed before our knowledge including all the forces that are determining, furthering or restricting our evolution. The spiritual order becomes clearly manfest to us. It is difficult to completely envisage all the advantages that follow the emergence of the psychic but this can be said that with its emergence we can have only a glimpse into but not active touch with the divine light. The Tantras in emphasising this psychic revelation envisage a new evolution of man into and the consummation of spirituality even far beyond that.

Psychic life has its elasticity. It can easily expand or contract itself. It has no inertness. It is more plastic than mind, and has quicker formations than mind. This power of quick formation acquaints us with its power of expansion or contraction. The mental formations are free within a range. It has its own laws which it cannot transcend. For example the mind is hedged round by the limitations of space and time. Its universe is a universe either in space or time, the mind cannot conceive a universe without them. Psychic perception goes beyond both space and time. It can make contraction of space and time and clearly demonstrates their relative character. They are true so long as our evolution is confined to its present height. The finer evolution of the psychic being shows that the barrier of space and time is not absolute.

Our vital intuition or mental intuition can not overstep the limits of space and time. They function within their bounds. The vital or mental expansion cannot envisage a state of existence in which the time-space limits are fully overcome. The mind cannot picture space in its un-dividedness, time in its integrity. It apprehends the division of space and time. It comprehends their distinctive difference. Total space and total time naturally remain to us a concept. It never becomes a percept. Hence philosophers like Bergson or Ouspensky speak of intuition as directly apprehending either the continuity of time or the continuity of space.

Bergson makes space unreal, Ouspensky makes time unreal. The one accepts time as real, other accepts space as real. None goes beyond them but develops the world process either from context of Time or of Space. They do this with the help of mental intuition. What is a faint shadow for mental intuition is a clear fact for psychic intuition. Psychic intuition oversteps the barrier of space and time. The division of time as past, present and future disappears, and the unrolling of existence in time appears as a myth. There is no division of the past, the present and the future. The past glides into the present, the present into the future, none can say how and when. Time, in the ordinary sense. then, is the creation of the mind. through memory and anticipation. With the psychic contraction and expansion the sense of its reality vanishes. The past, the present and the future simultaneously appear before consciousness in the Supra-mental time-sense. In other words, time-limitation is transcended. The transcendence gives us the greater freedom and expansion of conscious-being. What is philosophically conceived by the Absolutist e,g, (Bradley) is an actuality to the psychist, for he, by his psychic development, can actually see the contraction of time. Time passes into a timeless perception in the wide, comprehensive consciousness. The idea of motion also vanishes with time. Motion is always relative to two points in space and time. When consciousness becomes wide enough to reflect simultaneously the two points, the idea of motion and the idea of time vanish. The distant points are then perceived simultaneously. They are reflected at the same moment in the same centre. In the higher intuition there is the clear possibility to outstep the limitations and visualise the world in its sweep. Life-force is related to time, when it is on the point of expression. When it is contracted into an equilibrium it has no connexion with time.. To represent life-force as also time is to ignore its occasional equilibrium independent of time. This is true of the vital, the mental, and the psychic equilibrium. In fact our whole experience points to a timeless existence. What is true of time is also true of space. We have knowledge of spaces, but not of undivided space. Such knowledge is possible when one has cosmic consciousness. The abstract space of mathematics is a necessary axiomatic assumption, of which concrete experience is not claimed by the astronomers and the mathematicians. The mystic claims such concrete knowledge by psychic expansion or contraction. The distance in space is dissolved as soon as our consciousness enlarges itself and grows cosmic. Śaivaism accepts this conclusion when it holds that Kāla (time) represents the order of mental events.

Timeless perception has two meanings. It may mean the vanishing of Time completely. Emphasis is laid upon this kind of consciousness in mysticism. Mysticism stretches this transcendence of Time in the absolute stillness. This is a unique realisation beyond all spiritual stir. This is in the terminology of the Tantras the quietude of the Parama-Śiva. Timeless may also mean freedom beyond the triple divisions of the past, the present and the future and the presentation of continuity. This is the supramental-time consciousness beyond the mental perception of time. The supra-mental Time-sense presents time in its transcendent and creative formation without the least break in its continuity. It is the time-less perception of the process in time. The creative formation is continuous. The separateness of our mental perceptions is removed by the cosmic togetherness in which time in our sense does not function. It becomes the vehicle of expresssion in one continuous link without the emergence of the new or the withdrawal of the old. Time here moves on the wings of eternity, levelling down the individuality of the moments and fusing them in one sweeping whole.

Some kinds of mystical experience are a sufficient evidence of *psychological relativism*.. Our mystical experiences have many forms. Some are concrete experiences. The sudden flashes of exquisite beauties, the parade of radiant forms, the infusion of divine grace into the soul are experiences essentially concrete. They occur, the depths of being are stirred. Sometimes they give the impression of the possession by a great power, which lifts up their experiences to a height beyond concrete expression. Consciousness loses its grip on the thread of concrete experience. This transition from the concrete mystical experiences demonstrates the truth of psychological relativism, for ultimately such experiences are not absolute. They are variable, they are relative to our psychic constitution and build. The sensing of great power or force is an actual experience, but this power eventually helps the mystics to pass to a nobler realisation of peace and silence. Such experience is beyond concrete, mental or spiritual formations. The experience is preceded by the direct realisation of the contraction of space and time, the two great substratum of existence and experience. Mystics, as a class, feel the pressing urge to cross the bounds of space and time; and whatever their form of mysticism may be, it is clear that the demand of the seeking soul is fulfilled when the consciousness is free from the limitation of space and time. Mysticism is the sense of reassertion of consciousness in its freedom from spatial and temporal limitations. At this height human joys are overshadowed, the aesthetic and the moral beatitudes are left aside. Still this privilege the mystics cannot forgo, for it is really something unique.

Philosophers who are committed to thinking that knowledge implies the subject object relation in all can neither see the truth nor can they appreciate the value of such an experience. This overcoming of all the usual barriers between the individual and the absolute is the great accomplishment.* Some realists find an apparent inconsistency in the statement. When all is discovered in oneness, there is none to be aware of this oneness. 'It requires conscious self to be aware of this oneness. This is a commonplace criticism. The realist ignores the knowledge by identity. This knowledge is not the knowledge in the normal sense of the term, still it is knowledge. The relation may drop, even then there is knowledge. Realism is committed to the subject-object *axis* of knowledge. It cannot rise above it to appraise the higher life of knowledge by sympathy. The knowledge by sympathy is knowledge by identity. The absorption of the subject in the object enables us to see more of the object than to represent it in our mental consciousness by a relation. Indeed the usual working of our mind is so preoccupied with the subject-object

* Quoted by Prof. Dawes Hicks in his Hibbert Lectures.

relation that in common experience no side of the relation is suspended—this is natural and common. Occasionally the law subsides in us, and we have a unique experience. This tendency does not long persist and the mind slips back again to its usual centre of gravity. The mystics affirm that evolution in super-consciousness will make knowledge by identity normal. And it requires a finer development of the psychic consciousness. It is its ardent desire to see immediately the heart of things, without going through the usual process of knowing. The mystics claim direct, imme-diate knowledge without exercising in the least the rela-tional consciousness. They see. Such knowledge is rare. Its rarity is no ground of its falsity. It is difficult to follow the mystics unless the knowledge by sympathy is developed in us. Such a state of consciousness is often *incommunicable* for memory can not carry any impres-sion of it. That does not make the experience an illusion. It is repeated in the psychic being which adequately carries some impression of so glorious an experience. This psychic habit really becomes the urge to still finer evolution in consciousness, when such knowledge may become more permanent and durable. One must not forget the elasticity of psychic life. Psychic experiences can be repeated with ease. The relations drop at a certain stage when the psychic expansion or contraction puts one beyond rational knowledge

The concrete emergences are definite formations in relation to a particular context fulfilling a particular purpose in a particular aspect. These concrete emergences control the definite bent in the cosmic history and expression. These concrete emergences form the cosmic and the individual history, and they are easily intelliglble and plainly visible. The psychic mind sees their operation, influence and power. They are indeed the cosmic powers behind the formations. They are very interesting. In spiritual life, they cast light and send invisible help when the seeker is surrounded by enveloping darkness. The Tantras entertain spritual experiences; taking life-attitude as the basis, they embrace all shades of feeling that may be evoked in the functioning of spiritual consciousness.

Spirituality in the Tantras commences with the theistic attitude. It is natural, for the spiritual life is evoked by the inner sense of a helplessness and the urge for the greater and wider existence, the constant demand of the realisation of the finer values, and above all, the sense of security of being and freedom from the constant uncertainties of an evanescent existence. The theistic attitude confronts us at the threshold of our spiritual life, because in this attitude our normal experience with all its formations and implications is active. Religiosity has a demand to rise above this attitude, for the yearning soul resolves all experiences into an all-absorbing experience. The God-intoxicated soul sees God and nothing else; God in nature, God in the finite soul. Even theism idealises our experience, and sees the immanence of God in every thing. When the religious enthusiasm grows intense, the distance between God and nature, soul and God dissolves and this psychic unfoldment is necessary to realise the direct touch of the divine in us. Some form of psychic opening takes place in all spiritual realisation, specially when it goes beyond merely intellectual understanding. The direct contact with the spirit is possible when the psychic self is active. Then alone one enjoys the directness and the force of spirit in its transparence, affability, elasticity and luminosity.

CHAPTER XV.
SPIRITUALITY IN THE VEDANTA AND THE TANTRAS.

The Tantras differ from the Vedānta and the Sāṃkhya in their approach. The discipline in the Tantras is essentially a discipline of our central being in a way which can release consciousness from its limitation ; but this discipline is not essentially philosophic or logic or analytical. It is on the other hand essentially psychic. It is interesting because it discovers truth through the direct reading of the life-forces, through their finer modulations and activity and through the acquaintance with the unconscious.

Our life-force is connected with the central being. A barrier between them is established by the creation of an individuality which resists the continuous stream of Light and force from the central source. The Tantric discipline removes this creative individuality and directly connects it with the central being and cosmic consciousness. Its method lies in correct aspiration and the descent of force which removes the barrier created by individuality. This is the distinctive character of the discipline ; it has indeed been the chief source of its attraction. The psychic life is potential in us, it becomes active when divine aspiration moves our being. A psychiasation of our being with new osscilations is the result,

The realising spirit sees God everywhere, it becomes merged in him. This is a living realisation of the immament spirit. When the distinction is dissolved, this spiritual realisation rise to the height where the question of transcendence or immanence has no meaning. Pantheistic realisation is the precursor of mystical exaltation and is the border land between the theistic adoration and mystical exaltation. It indicates in spiritual consciousness an important departure from the normal to the super-normal with its intensiveness. It is no intoxication. Spiritual life indicates evolution of consciousness, and the urge is there is break the barrier that separates man and nature from God by a process of elimination of the partialities and the relativities and by the final acceptance of the Absolute. The final reach is attained here. In some cases the fruition takes the form of a dynamic identification with God by reinforcing our will and identifying it with the cosmic will and this is accepted by those that prefer the concrete play of spirit in the creative order. This implies more than an occasional infusion of the divine will into the human. It is a constant possession. Such kind of realisation may be called *dynamic Pantheism*. It makes activism more prominent in spiritual consciousness. Such identification is also a super normal experience and gives the form of activistic mysticism. Activistic mysticism conceives the mysterious infusion of power into our soul and the propelling of the whole of our being under the influence of this power. Sometimes the feeling is clear that one is being led by a mysterious influence beyond one's proper sphere and has the conviction of the magnification of one's being and faculties. The feeling eventually grows clear that one's perscnality is being constantly energised by such an invisible power. An infiux of energy actually takes place, a higher will works upon our will, in the presence of which, 'Our minds are as passive as the windsweptwaves'. It is not a very rare experience. It sets at ease the doubts entertained about it.

Dynamic spirituality differs both in form and inspiration from spiritual absorption or transcedence. Personality is not denied here, though at a stage the human personality is overshadowed by the higher will. Here also there is an absorption in which the ego is at its minimum existence, almost *nil,* but the personality is retained, for the concentration of force requires a medium and centre. In both ways the Tantras do not give to human personality the emphasis that is often laid upon it. Personality is a help as well as a bar, Spiritual inspiration in its intensity and height transforms it in such a way as that nothing human is left in it, for the natural aspiration to rise above the human and absorb and assimilate the divine in it. The trace of the human is an active reminder, but the unwillingness of the spirit to shake off personality is born of timidity that refuses to face the truth boldly. The old self still lingers and the new one is not yet born. Man does not know the dignity of the unborn soul. Fixed in its transcendence, the soul rises in cosmic rhythm and moves with the cosmic power.

Through the psychic the cosmic consciousness

directly acts upon our being and liberates it from its rigidity and restrained vision. It instils more energy into our vital being, it makes the mind intuitively more active; it discovers the centres which are directly exercised by the cosmic Will. The individual will is the cosmic will focussed in the centre. In its association it naturally becomes limited in being and operation. This limitation is to be removed.

This indeed is definite emergence of our being. The true nativity of man takes place when we invite the recreating force in us by going over our inherited tendencies and by removing narrow individuality. The Trantras make the individual ego the centre of the cosmic will, and therefore, the will in its humanistic sense is overshadowed. This loss is compensated by the power it acquires and by the guidance of the superior reason which it releases. The Tantras lift the veil from it.

In the super-conscious is stored up the fine spiritual powers which instil superb harmony into our vital and mental being. To this end, the Tantras instruct us to surrender ourselves completely to the promptings of the higher spiritual forces which further the evolution of our being.

Abstract spirituality which gives understanding, but does not face the actualities of life finds no important place in the Tantras. Here the problem is concrete—how to activate the immanental spirit in us. The Tāntric discipline unfolds the spiritual consciousness together with the spiritual power. It is illumination, but above all education and remoulding of our being. The

Tantras evoke graces and powers which can give us a taste for concrete spirituality. They discover the Sun-Lit path which can make life easy and beautiful and at the same time invest us with transcendental wisdom.

The Tantras accept the creative harmony ; and the psychic resonance of our being, as of spiritual value and significance. The Tantras do not ignore the fine poise in transcendence ; and as instrumental to it the dynamic being moves in consonance with spiritual harmony. The Sun-lit path does not ignore any side of our nature in spiritual realisation. By following the stream of light that occasionally visits us, the Tantras reach the highest consummation. They make the transcendent light reflect through the centres of our being, making them more powerful, graceful and easy. The Tantras give illumination but in addition, they make the most of life by drawing from the unconscious, and in evolving a course of life and expression in spirituality and grace.

The spiritual force is hidden in us and cannot be fully active because of the defective system. Before the spirit-force can be active fully, it introduces changes in our physiological and vital system to make it a fit vehicle of spirit. Then the cosmic sense and cosmic power grow in us. The veils of ignorace are lifted and the subtler layers of existence endowed with subtle forces become facts of clear knowledge. These indeed are indirect fruits of spiritual progress itself. The Tantric realisation makes room for varieties of spiritual experiences, the initiate is to make his progress through grades of being. These experiences have value showing the subtle forms of being and the subtle powers of consciousness, in higher planes. But these are smaller considerations before the end that is placed before us *viz.*, the realisation of the transcendent truth of *śiva*. The Tantras are often looked upon as the discipline which evokes uncommon powers in us. That is quite possible in as much as they make the central being active in the astral and still in the higher planes; but these powers are not the end that is consciously sought. In spiritual life the Tantras along with the tradition built up lay more stress on the attainment of the supreme light than the attainment of power. Powers are the natural consequences of unfettered being in knowledge.

With this aspiration the indrawing force reveals its many phases and produces infinite harmonies that make us fully acquainted with them. Defferent harmonies suit different psychic temperaments. The Tantras prescribe different paths for different individuals. This must be the case since the psychological moulding takes distinct shapes according to inherited tendencies, and individuality. The great art in spiritual life is to suit our mental and psychic constitution to the different kinds of spiritual modulations. The Tantras allow our spiritual nature to assert itself by completely surrendering our being. The spiritual surrender does not produce a merely negative state, it evokes gentle spiritual currents in consonance with our psychic being.

Owing to this, it has been made possible for the Tantras to assimilate love, power, and wisdom in spiritual life and to embrace all kinds of spiritual attitudes either in love or in wisdom. These attitudes become dominant according to our psychic formation. Generally the Tantras give the order as love, power and wisdom. Love gives the dynamic identification whence emerge power and wisdom. The Tantric mysticism indicates different phases in response to the definite modulations. Occultism has different shades. It is not definitely fixed for a particular experience. It stands for the delicate experiences associated with the spiritual tremor of our being. But this does not mean that all spiritual experiences have the same value and potentiality. The spiritual tremor is felt through our vital-mental and higher mental being. It rejuvenates them and produces pleasing vibrations, but the vibrations that emanate from the depth and the height of our being have greater value because they touch the higher spring of life. Their great contribution lies in withdrawing the barrier of matter and making life more shapely by drawing directly from the creative force. By evoking the cosmic creative will, the Tantras displace the determinism of nature and establish the indeterminism of spirit. This does not remain a philosophic concept, this becomes an actual fact in life.

This consummation becomes possible because the Tantras realise in the 'Mahā-Śakti' (transcendent will) the power to eventually dispense with the supposed antagonism of matter and spirit and to spiritualise matter. Matter is more a convention than acceptance. It has no reality. It originates out of the creative will in the process of emergence. It cannot sufficiently resist the creative will. The creative will has in it potency to re-shape mind and matter for more exalted expression. The emergence of a new creative order is possible and the Tantras work in this direction.

It would be the height of indiscretion to suppose that the Tantras are discliplines in will-culture in the modern sense. The training of will makes will effecttive, but does not make it one with the cosmic will. The Tantras give the finest act of evoking the cosmic will in us which alone possesses the power of re orienting our being. The trained will has not this power. To move the divine force in us, to regulate all the centres of our being by it makes our being elastic, fit for a still higher emergence in spirituality, wisdom and power. This becomes possible because matter, life, and mind emerge in finer existence by the pressure of the creative spirit. Evolution is the assertion of spirit over nature. Matter is de-materialised and the creative will becomes highly active to work out the cosmic possibilities in man.

The concrete spirituality of the Tantras acquaints us with these exhalted possibilities. The divinisation of our being is the Tāntric ideal ; though the transcendence has not been ignored, still the Tantras, specially as an applied art in spirituality have removed the barrier between man and God, by the elimination of the earthly bent, born of ignorance. The Tantras have accepted matter, but practically have eliminated it by redeeming life from its influence. In the Vedānta the identification of the human and the divine will has been supposed to be inferior to transcendence. The Tantras have worked out more thoroughly the process of activism of the divine will in man. Our psychic being is so influenced that our divine possibilities are actualised and a new consciousness with new powers is directly established. The whole being moves with a new tempo. Spiritual life is opposed to the life of concentration. The freedom from the restricted movement and expression is its keynote and essence.

Both the Sāṁkhya and the Vedānta avoid dynamic spirituality, because they do not accept the dynamical principle to be spiritual. No doubt, the Vedānta admitted the fellowship with the divine by inviting the dynamical urge indicated in the Ahaṁgraha-Upāsanā; but, strictly speaking, this pseudo-spirituality leaves one in the half-way house on the path of illumination. It is identity with the cosmic will. That decidedly is a luminous experience vivid and rich in chastened feeling and irresistible movement; but that cannot put us beyond the relativity of experience and adaptation.

The Sāṁkhya and the Vedānta realise the necessity of extreme detachment from the felicities and subtle presentations that attend the chastened and disciplined being. The supreme puissance of Transcendence cannot be attained, if there is the least ripple in our dynamic being. In the life of spirit there is the necessity of maintaining an even attitude towards all fruitions in order that the central motive be not lost sight of, the escape from becoming into Being. To this end, the philosophic conviction of the Transcendence of reality and being together with clear differential consciousness of Being and becoming is surely helpful. The conviction, the discrimination, and the difference in the sense of values make for final realisation.

The Vedānta and the Yoga system conceive a world of greater spiritual values and prescribe the course for the adepts who retain personality and self-consciousness. Here the adepts pass through the subtler expressions of life and consciousness, finally reaching the highest spiritual plane of existence in Brahma-Loka. This path is called *Deva Yāna,* the path of shining light, following which no body returns again to human existence. The path is known to the mystics. It proceeds from the heart-cave to the abode in the core of the brain and finally to the finer layers of spiritual existence arranged in heirarchy. The adepts become suffused in heavenly light and power and become free from earthly clingings. Streams of light enter into their being and finally they get direct access into the Brahma-Loka, the region of unbounded and serene light. This is the path of spiritual evolution as distinct from the path of direct illumination and wisdom. In this path also the final illumination is attained if the adept seeks it. But the process is the same, the path of final discrimination of the Puruṣa from the Prakṛti. Patañjali retains the distinction between the individual Puruṣa aspiring for the spiritual liberation and Iśvara. They are distincts. The Vedānta maintains a kind of dynamic identification between the aspiring soul and Iśvara and enjoins certain spiritual fruitions accessory to those that enjoy the same orbit of existence *e.g.*, the intensity in power, and wideness in knowledge. But for the final consumation detachment from the divine felicities are to be cultivated. Patañjali in the *Vibhūti Yoga* enumerates the list of supra-human powers that an adept attains, but these powers exhibit the truth that in the spiritual evolution the control over Prakṛti is possible in all cases, and is assuredly attained in some cases. But here the path is not finished, and finer adaptation leads on to Illuminative Calm.

This requires a qualification. Creativity implies concentration of Spirit. Spirituality implies diffusion of spirit.

Spirituality in the Tantras stands in inverse relation to creativity. Spirituality is the contrary movement proceeding from the definite to the indefinite. The first step is to go beyond the definite formation in the creative order in the Sadvidyā.

Sadvidyā marks a definite stage in the process of concentration of the supreme principle. Through the process of concentration and synthesis, it objectifies itself as the primary will, 'I am this'. When this stage is attained the finite individuality is lost and the finite subject experiences the supra-individual subjectivity. In the spiritual ascent, the adept goes beyond the realm of Prakṛti, and by cultivating dynamic identity with the basic principle, it overcomes the limitation of its nature. The Sadvidyā is accession into over-mental consciousness, where the knowledge-will is released from its limitation of the finite self. It is related to the still higher ranges and indefinite expansion of Being. It is intermediate between the supreme heights of Being and the creative existence.

Naturally Satvidyā is a stage in advance of Patañjali's Vivekaja Jñāna. It is a kind of immediate knowledge which reveals elements of existence (emergent evolutes, and their relation) in the high frequency of psychic knowledge which otherwise escapes notice. It is knowledge which overrides the limitations of time-succession and reflects the objects immediately, directly, simultaneously as a powerful reflector. In spiritual life it has a value as it reflects the total creative existence indicating an advance over the piece-meal knowledge of a fettered consciousness. But still this knowledge does not go beyond the definite formation in creative order and can not reflect the greater heights of knowledge in Satvidyā. 'Vivekaja Jñānam' is confined to the creative order. Satvidyā transcends the order of creative formation.

The next step in realisation is Iśwara. Iśwara is represented as a definite stage in the ascending order beyond Sadvidyā in which the objective element not-'I' in the dialectic process becomes more dominant. This process of objectification is more marked. The definite synthesis in Sadvidyā is not possible without this objectification. Synthesis is possible when two sides, the subjective and the objective, are well represented and fully drawn out. Spirituality in this phase is diffusive. Spirit radiates its influence and scatters it to Not-self. This represents the Iśwara Tattva. Next in the order of ascent is Sadāśiva-Tattva. The definite will is here mainfested. It is the stage of transition between the transcendence of Śiva and the definite concentration of Iśwara. It is where expression in definiteness takes its initial start. It is primordial will which is not altogether without any objective reference. Its object is not so distinct as that of knowledge'.... (Pandey. Abhinava Gupta). It is the stage of will prior to the objectification of will. Spirituality in this stage is the recoiling of spirit upon itself enjoying the tendency to definiteness in expression. Beyond this is the still higher stage where all primordial definiteness as represented in Sadvidyā disappears and the spirit enjoys its perfect poise and the equilibrium in the recoiling of Śakti in Śiva, the stillness of becoming in the wideness of being. These stages are to be passed through before the adept realises the final transcendence and identity.

It should not be lost upon us that in the rarefied heights of supreme experience there is no contrariety of synthesis involved in dialectic process. The process is supralogical. For the whole movement is the inward expression of spirit in which there is no correlatives but only the degrees of conceptual expression. The intensity of concentration determines its grade of existence. Sadāśiva enjoined the highest diffussion of Being—It is being in its utmost expression. ParamaŚiva has no expansion or concentration.

Sadvidyā represents the nodus of the unity of the higher ranges in spiritual expression with the creative expression of the Prakṛti. It is a point which marks out the definite formation and expression of the transcendent reality in its descent; this definiteness allows it a direct connection with Prakṛti. The orders of expression beyond Sadvidyā are nebulous, wide and vast. Consciousness and will in these do not emerge into that definite expression and concrete play which can allow its descent into the lower orders of creative Prakṛti-mind, life and matter. The spiritual infusion into the lower orders proceeds from the Sadvidyā. The spiritual potency assumes here such intuitive concentration as can make it effective and influence mind, life, and matter. It is the concentrated light of the spiritual sun which illumines our life and consciousness. The wider, the vaster, the the serener light of the above is reflected through this medium which relates it to the still dimmer light of our consciousness. Its will and force relates itself to the feebler will and life. This way Sadvidyā has influence not merely as focussing a definite synthesis or concrete unity, but as representing a stage in expression which can focuss in itself the diffused light of spirit. It is the centre wherefrom spiritual light emerges in its soft and mellowed lustre, in its absorbing beauty, in its concrete afflorescence. It is the centre where the divine will exhibits itself in its redeeming power. It is where the divine-knowledge-will makes its unmistakable impress and is felt as actively shaping and influencing the spiritual order in the cosmos by the emergence and emanation of spiritual powers.

Sadvidyā can be favourably compared to Śrī Auravindo's over mind. 'It covers us with wide beings of some creative over soul. It covers the whole lower hemisphere of knowledge-ignorance, links it with the greater truth-consciousness, while at the same time with its brilliant golden lid, it veils the face of greater truth from our sight,......It is at once a passage and an obstacle in our seeking of the spiritual existence and its secret reality.

The experience of the Sadvidyā is concrete unity where the subject and the object are distinct, but united as indivisible moments in the same Being. This concrete unity of the subject and the object is not evident in the lower stage of Vidyā (knowledge) where the distinctness of the subject and the object is more emphasised than its unity. It is therefore, the divided presentations of experiences peculiar to our unillumined knowledge and un-inspired life. Naturally our life and spirituality have also a narrow significance. They are cut off from the concentrated light of Sadvidyā and howevermuch it may strive to assert the spiritual life and to reflect the spiritual light, it can hardly do so with success. It does not allow that evenness of Being which can penetrate into the unity of consciousness of the Sadvidyā. Naturally the Spiritual seedling begins in the Sadvidyā stage. Even the discriminating consciousness of I as laid down in the Sāṁkhya is not recognised by the Kashmir Saivaism as spiritual, for it emphasises distinction and not integrity, Concrete spirituality is more unification than discrimination in which the "I" and "not I" are held in balance. Spirit is assimilating and embracing. It is not the denial or refusal.

The realism of the creative order which the Sāṁkhya maintains and the unconscious purposiveness with which the creative principle functions have been modified by the Tantras, specially by the Kashmir Saivaism, to suit their setting not by denying the creative principle, but by affiliating it to the supreme transcendent consciring. Hence it has been possible for the Tantras to retain spiritual felicities along with spiritual transcendence.

In the Tantras the dynamic spiritual felicities have meaning and reality in the order of spiritual values for they are affiliated to reality and expression. The synthesis in the Sadvidyā represents a definite phase in concreteness through the inherent force of dialectic and it should not be mixed up with the initial being—becoming which has no concrete form. In Tantricism becoming is not the synthesis of being and not-being It is one with Being. Not-being is not recognised as a category contrary to being.

The Tantras emphasise over-mental spirituality beyond the creative expression. With this is experienceed a release from the sense of restraint, and an unbounded ease and spontaneity. The adept is raised to the over-mental planes, before he can pass beyond all definite formation into Transcendent calm.

CHAPTER XVI.

THE COLLECTIVE SPIRITUALITY

The Vedānta primarily is discipline in self-realisation; its greatest achievement is the knowledge of self, (Swarājya-Siddhi). The Tantras along with this establishes the kingdom of spirit on earth. Spiritual illumination scatters its radiance. By its affiliating power it captivates and attracts. The Tantras emphasise liberation as well as collective Spirituality through radiation of spirit. They give power which forms spiritual centres; the finely attuned natures become the centres of vast spiritual influence which can usher in new cycles of spiritual expression.

This possibility is inherent in spiritual realisation. The Vedānta by its emphasise upon Transcendence is not keen about it; though a radiance is transmited from all spiritually awakened souls, still nothing actively is done to usher in a new expression. The Vedantic adepts are more for self-liberation than for establishing a reign of spirituality and a spiritual hegemony. Its passion is to pass into ineffable light. The Tantras, on the other hand, take up the organisation and the spiritualisation of society by infusing spiritual power and light into the constituent members. The collective spirituality is the definite ideal in the Tantras. Spiritual life gives clear evidence of the integrity of humanity and every advanced step in realisation brings home this truth to us. The Tantras establish society on a spiritual basis by eliminating the sense of separateness. Society is a spiritual order. The Tantras make the spiritual basis of society more alive in us by exalting

'One interior life
In which all beings live with God, themselves,
Are God, existing in the mighty whole.'

The individual life reaches a height whence it can feel its spiritual identification with all and sees in the whole the reflection of the cosmic spirit. This impelling of the cosmic spirit becomes active in us and naturally the sense of individuality emphasising individual liberation is displayed by universalism. The collective redemption is a great spiritual promise. Knowledge gives individual redemption. Love works for collective redemption. The Tantras keep these two efforts active in us. Knowledge makes love possible. The freedom of transcendence is not eclipsed. The release from partial existence in transcendence activates life-force in spirituality. Every step in higher realisation makes us fill the wider dimension of being and the commanalty of spirit and naturally the sense of integration becomes keenly alive.

The concrete inspiration of the Tantras invigorates the life-force in society and induces collective thinking and spirituality. This enthusiasm is followed to the extent of spiritualising all the active expression of life. Indeed the Tantras have refused to accept the isolation of spirit and to seek its liberation by dissociating itself from matter. The attempt has been essentially made to re-affirm spirit through all the movements of life in order that its finer integration and expression may be established. To this end, the Tantras re-shaped all the forces and re-orient their relation. These are apparently the functioning of the different forces........but the Tantras affiliate them to the spiritual force.

The Tantras establish our life relations and expression on the basis of spirituality. A spiritual order in the family and society is the natural consequence of such aspiration. The Tantras boldly meet the conflict and contraries of life and discover the deeper currents of spirit in which they completely melt away. They set aside the conflict of nature and spirit, of individual and society, of the sexes by discovering in the heart of things a deeper harmony of spirit. Spirit creates antagonism for its expression and spirit transcends it. This is the play. There is no *how* or *why* of it.

The creative values are essentially spiritual and not merely moral. The Tantras with deeper insight transcend the moral values and the conflicts associated with them and finds out the spiritual values which can bring together the ugly and beautiful, the evil and the good and harmonise them in the life of spirit. The moral personality which emerges from the contradiction of our nature and the assertion of spirit over nature is overshadowed in the spiritual realisation where the tension is removed. Moral life is displaced by spiritual life. Moral life has tension. Spiritual life has no tension. Spirit resolves conflicts by its transforming vision and power. The humanistic standard of valuation is overshadowed by the divine standard, wherein the human values lose their significance and relative verities lose their power. The Tantras regulate life by spiritual valuation. Spiritual urges are cosmic and are not determined by ethical values. Spirit is a-moral or supramoral. Moral values are social conventions. Even when they are accepted as creative ideals, they are emergences and mental constructs. Spirit goes beyond the mind and the values or ideals afforded by them will be essentially different from those conceived or created by our mind. The Tantras regulate life relations by spiritual ideals and are not limited by the dualities which govern the mental pursuit of an ideal. The idea of 'Holy' remains an objective ideal but cannot be fully assimilated. Moral life always supposes a distance between the ideal and the actual, and if this divergence is removed, it loses its character. Even in perfect realisation this distance will not be absorbed.

Quite different is *spirituality*. It means always the over-coming of this tension between the ideal and the actual. The ideal is identified with life-force. A complete dynamic identification is established between the spirit and the creative self. In Spiritual life, the previous habits of thoughts and urges of life are discarded for new expressions. It is essentially education of spirit, and spirit surmounts human moral codes. Spiritual life is no definite attainment. It is essentially being, naturally dynamic identification oversteps the divergence between the ideal and the actual which is the ground of our moral valuation and existence. Spiritual life is not an effort of actualising the ideal, for it really transcends the order of values and seeks identification with reality. In the ascent, the order of holiness, the orders of radiant existences, may directly cross our views, and come to our help, but the consummation is reached in being identified with the basic reality. The Tantras surpass the relativism that is associated with moral and spiritual values. Tantricism emphasies the identification with the transcendent will as the spiritual ideal at a certain stage. Anyhow the spiritual effort is directed to overcome the joys and delights of personal self, to free consciousness from its limitations and to enjoy its unlimited being and power. The human self becomes dynamically one with the cosmic will and power.

The spiritual orders are established by the diffusion of spiritual force through the psychic centres. They can help a new cycle of evolution in spirituality by radiating such influence. When one particular centre is inspired it saturates its surroundings with its influence and creates a kind of electromagnetic spiritual field. The Tantras lay special emphasis upon establishing a collective spirituality and spiritual expression by directly contracting with the centre. The other centres seek a dynamic identification with the central figure by quiet passivity. This way an equilibrium is established amongst a group of souls which feels an equal elasticity and expression of being. This equilibrium is made possible by encountering a negativity amongst the less developed souls which then draw from the positive centre. A negative centre is the Anima, it has drawing and attracting power. This helps to maintain perfect equilibrium between the active and the receptive centres. A spiritual poise is enjoyed. Without the former, the latter has no existence, without the latter the former has no expression. The Tantras apply this principle of distinction in identity in concrete spiritual life and this explains its rich and varied expression. The Tantras actually help collective liberation by the power of radiation and emergence of spiritual force. And in emphasising dynamical spirituality, the Tantras have helped a collective expression in spirituality. This does not mean deflection from the centre,......this is only a spreading out of the spiritual force which evolves finer types of humanity. This affiliation of active with passive spirituality gives fullness in spiritual life—grace, majesty and peace. The Anima is brought under the complete control of the Animus which changes its nature under its influence. The conflict between the two sides of our nature must be eliminated, and this is done by spiritualising the Anima. The ideal nature is not lost, but the Anima soon shows exhibition of the softer qualities in spiritual life,—by absorbing the spirit in it. A spiritual communism thus grows and is established through collective spirituality. This collective spirituality becomes possible because of the radiation of the forces of knowledge, love and power. Each centre in the spiritual commune becomes a centre of living force. The formation is spontaneous ; it is done by the affiliating force of spirit.

CHAPTER XVII.

THE YOGA OF KUṆḌALINĪ :—

The Tantras place great emphasis upon the Yoga of Kuṇḍalinī. It is their unique discovery.

Kuṇḍalinī is the great spiritual power hidden in man. It is so called because of its coiled nature. (The word 'Kuṇḍala' means 'Coiling' as the coiling up of a serpent. It is supposed to be stored up at the end of the spinal chord). (*Ahīsadṛśakṛt*). Kuṇḍalinī is reserve force. The word 'coiled up' has that implication. This force is psychic and spiritual. It has its effect upon the vital force, even upon our physical being. This force is not confined to man alone. It is potential everywhere. Only in man it is effective. Kuṇḍalinī is a cosmic principle. It is everywhere, even in an atom of matter. The operative power in comparison with the reserve force is a drop in the ocean. Kuṇḍalinī is the primal force or Śakti involved in all existence. We can move it for further evolution. It is the immanent force or will to help higher ascents in evolution and therefore its importance in our higher unfolding is so great. It exists as a potential power, the whole spiritual art lies in making this power active. It gives spiritual fecundation. Generally it is felt as a subtle current of energy which is luminous, and which follows through a subtle passage in our system, but the current is not necessarily confined to it, it penetrates into the finer ethereal expansion far above our physical being. 'It is', says, Sāradātilaka 'like a flash of lightning' (Vidyutlatākāra). It is really the higher urge for a better evolution in wider being and consciousness. When Kuṇḍalinī remains inactive man acts with his normal strength and knowledge but with the awakening of Kuṇḍalinī, he acquires super-human strength and power. Kuṇḍalinī generates a force which unearths our whole being in order that it may really implant a new consciousness and infuse a new life. It is nothing miraculous, but the use of a great gift that is already in man in order that man may supersede his present stature in being and knowledge and can acquire new knowledge and power and put them into active service for a divine purpose. It acquaints us with the still unborn self, the self which is our real nature and essence. Spiritural life is essentially the seeking of this unborn self, for the evolutionary ascent has not been completed with man. The evolutionary urge is still for higher manifestation, where man will be relieved of his limitations of knowledge and power. With the stir of Kuṇḍalinī the true spiritual evolution starts. Many undreamt of possibilities unfold. It will be possibly a mistake to suppose that the Yoga of Kuṇḍalinī constitutes in itself a new art or discipline. In every form of spiritual discipline, the Kuṇḍalinī is active. Whenever there is a poise in our being either through love or knowledge or Yoga, Kuṇḍalinī stirs, though at times not to our knowledge. Super-conscious realisation is the direct effect of this force. It is the released force of spirit, weaving new feelings, opening new vistas, starting freshness, yielding serene joys, unfolding our divine nature.

The Tantras, more than other forms of Indian Mysticism, strive to awaken Kuṇḍalinī and regulate it in order that the highest fruit may be reaped.

(*a*) *Life process and Kuṇḍalinī* :-

Kuṇḍalinī is active more or less everywhere in all life. Kuṇḍalinī is in beings in all grades of existence. Its finest functioning is seen in spiritual genius, where its flow, radiation and saturation are matters of direct perception. With the entrance and initiation into spiritual life, its finest stirring can be consciously felt, and spiritual life becomes so attractive because of the new vital and the conscious force it releases. The Life process is quickned by Kuṇḍalinī. And naturally it may so fashion and guide our life-force that it may appear more gentle, intense, lovely and joyous. It gathers up great force and makes its finest exhibition in spiritual formation and creativeness. It removes the barrier of normal consciousness and invests it with a rare luminosity and power. In fact, the life process is so much quickned by Kuṇḍalinī that it takes many forms of expression in knowledge, emotion and spirituality. It fills our whole being and modulates all the chords. If Kuṇḍalinī invests us with new life, it also endows us with new knowledge. To say that Kuṇḍalinī develops our intuition is not to say enough. It makes our intuition swift; but what is more, it associates new knowledge with new life; it quickens our intuitions in all its phases, for its purpose is to lay bare all the higher potentialities in vitalism, in psychism and spiritualism. Naturally with the functioning of Kuṇḍalinī, a new spirit-force along with new intuition in the higher grades of consciousness become active in us. Its whole movement is cosmic. Even in its sproutings, it gives an inkling into the cosmic ways of life. It invests actual existence with a new meaning and interest as it enables us to see it directly in the cosmic setting, not only in its totality, but in its integral unity with the universal life and consciousness. It actually saturates us with universal life- force and fills us with serene consciousness

Naturally with its awakening a new subtle order of knowledge starts, which is not possible to envisage, far less to understand with the functioning of the normal faculties. We are thrown into a universe in which we enjoy a finer being, wider knowledge, unfettered by the consciousness of three dimensions.

Kuṇḍalinī reveals the inner architecture of our psychic being together with the cosmic correspondence. It opens the avenues of subtler perceptions through the senses, suble mentalism and imaging, subtler vital harmonies, subtler beauties, and transcendental essence. It makes a new orientation of our being. The kind of intuition it generates is psychic, spiritual, supra-mental and transcendental. It makes our vital and mental being transparent. It makes the physical and the vital being sensitive to finer impacts and waves. A fresh vitality with a luminous psychism is the inevitable experience that follows the working of Kuṇḍalinī in us.

It is not the chastened animal spirit that attracts us here. It is not mere vital rejuvenation that awakens us. It gives us still deeper insight into our being and endows us with psychic intuition that puts us into connection with the subtle nature-spirit, natural agencies, denizens of heaven, and what is more, with cosmic emanations. It reveals its wonderous powers that are active to shape the nature of events and its inestimable gifts that acquaint us with the occult government of the world.

In whichever part of our being, Kuṇḍalinī becomes active, it reflects the forces that are operative there. It endows us with secret knowledge of its formation, and the forces and powers that are functioning there. Our system possesses fixed sensitive parts—they are focal centres which control and regulate certain forces in us. The powers of Kuṇḍalinī release these forces and make them active in us, endowing us with direct vision, subtle powers. All the centres do not give us the same kind of knowledge. Some give us the knowledge of the vital universe ; some the knowledge of the subtle mental universe, some still, of the finer universes. When it reaches the highest centre, it attains a dynamic equilibrium, and perfect poise and peace. It is the focal point in transcendental consciousness. The intermediate planes show all the possibilities of evolutions in spirit and subtle wisdom and mysteries of the different planes of our consciousness ; the highest plane manifests consciousness beyond all formations. It is the calm, the final reach of our being, and Kuṇḍalinī, when it reaches this zone, it gets widely diffused and attains perfect equilibrium. A unique experience in wideness and freedom persists.

Our being has sensitive psychic centres. They do not serve any physical function and generally they are inactive in us. These centres generate and diffuse currents of forces and become operative when the force of Kuṇḍalinī acts upon them. They are all located in the psychic body and Kuṇḍalinī makes the psychic self active in us.

The rise and the functioning of Kuṇḍalinī indicates the gradual psychication of our being. Evolution in knowledge and power proceeds even with imperfect psychication ; when the psychication becomes complete, divine wisdom and power are assimilated. Perfect psychication with complete spiritualisation will put the super-man in touch with the spring of divine life and he will be invested with cosmic consciousness and will. The type of super-man beçomes directly conscious of the divine power functioning in them and get identified with it. The awakening of Kuṇḍalinī invests us with psychic and cosmic forces.

All the principles of working are revealed when the spiritual force functions through all the centres. The promise is there, but life force works with accustomed habits and naturally it takes long before the cosmic powers can be directly active. In fact, no physiological or psychological analysis invests us with such knowledge. The details of our being are placed before us, and its physiological, vital, mental, psychic, supra-mental operations become clear to us, especially in their subtler and hidden aspects. These are but side-lights. The main objective is to endow us with the privilege of cosmic consciousness and freedom from limitations of the sense-mind and the vital impellings and the cabbined experiences. As the force starts, immediately the sense of expansiveness together with a freshness and vivacity fills us. This cosmic feeling is an invariable experience though it becomes clear and apparent when the experience has become some-what durable. All the centres do not give the same experience. Different centres have their distinctive psychic individuality, in as much as their functioning produces a different kind of vital feelings and psychic repose. Generally our system is divided into three parts, from the naval to the base, from the throat to the naval, from the brain to the throat. Vital experiences are quick and evident in the lowest part, vital-mental in the middle portion, the higher mental are located in the upper portion. This is at best a rough division, following the lead of usual experience, but in the case of adepts, the lower centres move in unison with the higher and gradually the lower centres lose their individuality by the process of transformation. Spirituality and occultism discover the immanent spirit through our nature. The immanence of spirit even in the vital life is clearly felt. This is indeed a great advance ; the crudeness of nature is eliminated before this advance is achieved. The latent forces of nature make their appearance ; they show their strength and power ; but all the powers of our being are linked up with the central spirit. A better organisation of forces takes place in us. The ideal is to mould our being in such a way that there can be no contradiction in different parts of our being. Each part submits to the influence of the higher force, and the physical, the vital, the mental centres part with their inertia, restriction, and formed habits and move in the wake of spirit. The apparent division that is noticed in our nature disappears. Throughout the whole being the creative spirit functions. The differences indicate their finer or crude functioning. Before the final release is attained, there is the emergence of the spirit in every part of our being in the physical, the vital, the mental, which refines our nature and enables us to react successfully to the cosmic functioning of spirit. This emergence in spiritual knowledge and spiritual power reaffirms the superiority of the spirit to matter and its ultimate control over it. The least advance is associated with freedom and ease. Each advance has its fruit in the attainment of magnified power and being called '*vibhūti*'. The Tantras along with Patañjali speak of varied powers which are far beyond the conception of the scientific intellect, for they follow the functioning of the subtlest forces; veils after veils are withdrawn and wonderous forces under the control of the released spirit are revealed endowing it with a form of superhuman omniscience. The emanation in powers is possible in the domain of Prakṛti, for the struggle between spirit and matter is possible, but beyond it there is no struggle in supra-material world, where the emanations are all spiritual. There is no extra-ordinariness in the exhibition of super-human knowledge and power. It is strictly determined by a law. The more the spirit re-asserts itself over matter, the more it throws out finer elements for its superior expression. With the functioning of Kuṇḍalinī the obstruction of inner matter is withdrawn from our sense, the heart, the intellect. The higher organs of our being then can function with more surety of results and with the directness of insight. This is the privilege that is associated with the rise of Kuṇḍalinī.

(*b*) *The Negative and Positive Pole of Existence* :—

There are two scales of our existence, the negative and the positive. Creation is the bi-furcation of the original unity of existence into a polarity. The polarity extends to knowledge, life and psychic processes. Here we speak of psychic and spiritual polarity—the division of the original force into a negative and positive form. This division really indicates the eccentric projection of the original force. In creation the projection gets a form of individuality and functions as such. It cannot immediately restore its original unity. Polarisation gives the stamp of concrete individuality by the balancing of the two forces, positive and negative. In some the positive force predominates, in others, the negative force dominates. Their nature and character are distinguished by these elements. There are also mixed types. The negative type is more intuitive and emotional, and more responsive to the finer currents of the soul. It is more subjectively conscious. The positive is creative, the negative is the receptive force, but the negative is not necessarily inferior for in the economy of life they have their own purpose to serve. The negative has in-drawing force, it attracts the positive which it in return fecundates. Thus arises the cycle of creation with two forms of psychism, negative and positive. Every created object has in it the two aspects of force, functioning in them. They determine its character. This bifurcation of force, though a natural process, is followed by another process *viz.*, depolarisation of forces. This is also natural in our life process, for in depolarisation the original unity is restored, and the forces enjoy equilibrium once again, before the process of creativity can, once again start. This alternate polarisation and depolarisation are evident in nature's functioning, nature manifests this way her creativity and economy. Activity and its suspension are at the root of all life-proceses.

Spiritual life begins with the freedom from the life of restriction implied in creative polarisation. It is, seriously speaking, not a life of transvaluation and conservation of values or a finer sense of aestheticism or a dignified Holiness. There are indeed all sublime expressions of life and consciousness, but they cannot forgo the very basis of personal existence. They cannot rise higher than the sense of values associated with personal life. Personal life is so intimately associated with religious consciousness that it is very difficult to think of spiritual life without a personal reference and personal feeling. But personality moves in a limited sphere; even at its height of expression it cannot rise above the limited reference to its centre. In other words, religion is the more dignified presentation of reality, always in relation to a personal reference. It is the focussing as it were, of the whole existence on a particular centre. Religion loses its charm if it misses this reference to expansive being and intensive feeling. This is, no doubt, a truism. But this is not the finality in our spiritual aspiration. The Tantras indulge in a form of spirituality which does not imply a passing into wider and higher reaches of consciousness, but a loss of the centre through which the spiritual experience appears to possess its correct meaning and proper value. This is the impersonal spiritual consciousness where the spirituality essentially is a process of depolarisation and is, therefore, an experience quite unique and different from the exalted sense of values and expanded being. This is a kind of supra-personal consciousness, beyond the cosmical feelings associated with the perception of cosmical existence.

The Yoga of Kuṇḍalinī moves the fibres of our existence so powerfully that our knowledge moves from the personal to the cosmical, and finally to the supra-cosmical. It acquaints us with these stretches of being and invests us with altogether a new form of knowledge whence vanishes the sense of relativity which characterises our normal consciousness. Kuṇḍalinī gives us this freedom. And naturally the spiritual life is above humanism or even super-humanism and the values associated with it and is intimately connected with investing our being with cosmic and supra-cosmic reality. At a certain stage in the evolution of spirituality the personal sense is overcome, and the cosmic and supra-cosmic sense opens, wherefrom it is possible to descend to the personal to elevate the collective consciousness to the cosmic and the supra-cosmic. This becomes possible when the sleeping force becomes active and rises upwards. The negative becomes united with the positive, complete equilibrium is reached. The inevitable experience is the widening of consciousness with fresh and quickened vitality. This is only the initial sign of the inception. A kind of fluid force is discharged and spreads over the whole system. As the force rises up, it invests every centre of existence with light and power. They become active cosmically.

(c) *The Music and the Colour of Kuṇḍalinī* :—

As Kuṇḍalini vibrates, wonderful symphonies are experienced. (*Kujanti Kuṇḍalinī*). A soft music and engrossing colour fill us. These are immediately experienced with its inception. It vibrates the universal life-force in us, bringing in its train the procession of music and colours. A perfect harmony with delicate ripples in form and sound is our immediate experience. The music and the colours and the fire of Kuṇḍalinī make us know 'what life is'. The mist of ignorance disappears; a new power of seeing into the heart of things and of hearing the delight-ful flood of music is acquired. The senses become gently modulated, receiving finer vibrations. The whole being stands in a fountain of flame. All seem clothed with colour and drenched with sound. There is a voice of stillness.

There is a light in darkness ; Kuṇḍalinī speaks through the voice of stillness, Kuṇḍalinī shines through the light of darkness.

In the perfect clarity of silence, the inaudible voice becomes audible, the invisible colour becomes visible. The one fills us with its delightful cadence, the other with soft impression. It develops intensive power of seeing and hearing, feeling and intuition. These are the greatest gifts of Kunṇḍalinī. It endows us with a new faculty which over-rides the spatial and temporal limitations.

The Tantras lend support to the emergence of a new sense, a new dimension of consciousness. It is no new evolution. It makes one thing definitely clear that there is no absolute distinction between the natural and supra-natural, for the Tantras do not accept any principle but creative spirit. In its ascent, the limitations of nature are removed and the creative spirit is revealed in super-natural expression, where a subtler spiritual order makes its appearance and psychic currents and events are directly felt and experienced.

This is the occult order, and the Kuṇḍalinī Yoga indirectly acquaints us also with it.

(*d*) *Spiritualism and Transcendence.*

Though the ascent of Kuṇḍalinī endows us with a fine psychic being with all its powers and possibilities acquanting us with the direct impress of spirit and starting a unique life in the divine beatitude and harmony yet the Tantras have assessed the highest of spirituality in transcendence, where the creative dynamism of spirit is replaced by the spirit in its non-creative transcendence. The Tantras characterise this state as beyond the realisation of the Godhead. Sometimes it is described as passing into the cloud of the unknowing, because it is something which can never be exactly described in terms of our experience, either intellectual or emotional—it defies all description. The Tantras conceive such exaltation in the highest intensity of mystical consciousness.

(*e*) *Kuṇḍalinī and Cosmic Harmonies* :—

With the rise of Kṇḍalinī our being beats in rapturous harmonies. These are not all subjective. Some of them are objective. Sometimes they give us super-human insight into the divine working of the world.

The Tantras lay special emphasis upon the acquaintance with these cosmic powers. The final spiritual objective is to be reached not by neglecting the dynamic possibilities, but by exhibiting them in their fullest extent and utilising them to the enrichment of life. They are welcome not in the sense of spiritual pragmatism, but in the effect of acquainting us with the truth of dynamic spirituality.

The path of the Tantras is not the path of renunciation; it is the path of a fuller and completer life, existence and finally of transcendence. The cosmic powers are such as can grant us supra-mental wisdom, power and vision and finally transcendence. A divine peotry, a divine philosophy, a divine art are amongst the possible fruitions ; in short the Tantras work out the hidden divine fecundities of life and give expression to its divine nature by fully working out its evolution by the help of the powers that lay hidden in it

This evolution is not otherwise possible. The Tantras, therefore, evoke the supra-natural powers and push evolution to a super-humanity, by seizing on the cosmic harmonies and by instilling them throughout our being in order that the hidden vital and psychic forces may be active in the higher spiritual evolution.

Hindu Psychology conceives these forces as 'Anna' (Physical) 'Prāṇa' (vital) 'Mana' (Mental) 'Vijnana' (Higher Mental), 'Ānanda' (Bliss) arranged in order and corresponding to them are their cosmic counterparts. The forces are psychophysical. The psychical and the physical are not completely different as they are often supposed. The psychical is the finer expression of the physical, or the physical is the dim expression of the psychical. The physical in the sense of crude existence has not been conceived; both the physical and the psychical are the forces which emerge out in the process of individuation of the divine will. They differ only in the degrees of condensation.

This indeed is bare psychology; it becomes a complicated process when the emergence of the different forces are traced out of the original will in the order of evolution; human evolution comes last and naturally in it all the forces exhibit themselves. The hidden psychology makes a searching analysis of our mental states by reference to these elemental forces and their psychic counterparts. It has been worked out fully in the Tantras. Every subtle movement in our make up, is traced to the original causes, either in the physical, or the vital, or in the higher forces. The elemental forces are the effects of these forces. The Tantras, therefore, locate at psychic centres different feelings and cognitions. Our feelings, emotions, agitations are analysed into these mysterious forces ; and, by regulating them changes and even transformations are introduced into them. The correspondence of the physical and the psychical are worked out throughout all the grades of our consciousness and the subtle line of connexion is traced between them and the original creative force. The connexion is traced between the different psychic centres and their modulations by the cosmic forces and can not be understood unless the Kuṇḍalinī functions. The occult psychology is revealed to us. Animal and human psychology is replaced by a spiritual psychology. The human ways and instincts are not rejected, but are better understood and their spiritual sense or meaning is appreciated. All the movements of our being, from whatever part they emerge are ultimately connected with the centre of inspiration. The Tantras anticipate physiological psychology in the explanation of diverse human behaviour ; but human behaviour comprises a vast field and all of them especially the subtle spiritual movements emerging from a plane higher than the vital or the physical or even the mental cannot possibly be explained in terms of ordinary human psychology, no matter, whatever be the type. Even the Tantras affirm that the lower centres have a connexion with the higher spiritual centres and when the occult insight opens the direct connexion between them can be felt. Complete spirituality strikes this higher evolution where the physical, the vital, and the mental forsake their normal ways. The animal and the human instincts change their nature and character under the pressure of higher force. Indeed it is the bold assertion of the Tantras that the spiritual is immanent in the physical and the vital. Under the domination of the spirit these forces exhibit finer expressions and change their character. When the spirit-force has been established in all the parts of being, the limitation of our being is removed and a new meaning, a new order of spiritual values, a new life-current and expression, a radiant beauty becomes apparent. Such is the vast possibility that is inherent in us; and the applied Tantricism is an art to move the sleeping forces in us in order that our spiritual evolution may be furthered not only to realise the transcendent calm, but also usher in a new order of supra-human evolution and to create a race of super men. The Tantras conceive occult hierarchies. They are actual existences. They attain this evolutionary height, by spiritual discipline. Our existence is inextricably blended and the elders on the path send helpful light to us by emmitting unconscious influence. (*Vide* different types of *Gurus* given in the Paraśurāma Kalpa Sūtra).

(f) *The Centres of Kuṇḍalinī* :—

Generally it is held that psychic force or better psychic fire is rooted at the base of the spine. The reservoir of force is there. And it rises upward from that centre. But the more accurate description will be that Kuṇḍalinī is everywhere ; it may stir up anywhere ; the particular centre where its first awakening will be felt depends upon the special responsiveness of a particular centre, provided that our being in those parts is free from complexities. Kuṇḍalinī introduces us into the unconscious. It withdraws the veil of the unconscious and leaves open its vast vistas. The experiences of luminosity, wideness and clarity always follow the stirring of the Kuṇḍalinī and naturally it must introduce us to the part of the unconscious which certainly is not what Freud calls the 'Id'. The 'Id' of Freud 'contains the passions'. It is the unconscious connected with the desires and with the vital life. The unconscious which becomes active with Kuṇḍalinī is free from the impetuousity of the vital life. It gives the feeling of a mental and vital plasticity, suppleness and ease. This is the general feeling with all the parts of being. When the Kuṇḍalinī functions, the sense of freedom from the ego-sense is evident. 'The Ego' says Freud 'represents what we call reason and sanity'. Correctly enough the freedom from the ego-sense establishes the greater sanity which follows the cosmic insight into things. Kuṇḍalinī really connects us with the super-ego which stands behind these layers of being and which draws inspirations from the hieghts of cosmical and super-cosmical existence. The 'unconscious' here is quite different from the unconscious of modern psychology. Better sense prevails with Freud when he says, 'That not only what is lowest, but also what is highest in the ego can be unconscious'. (page 33, The Ego and the Id.)

This unconscious embraces the vital, the psychic, the spiritual life, not only in their individual but in their cosmic import. But nowhere, are to be found the complexities of the normal or abnormal vital life. This implies that Kuṇḍalinī introduces us to the super-normal consciousness, putting us into relation with the cosmic vital, the cosmic psychic, the cosmic spiritual. These experiences have a special rythm in them, exhibiting their best form and style. Consciousness in such layers is free from the ego-reference and enjoys a freedom from the persistent urges of attending to the demands of objective life. Such experiences are not subjective, as they are indifferent to all personal satisfactions. Kuṇḍalinī, naturally offers a new consciousness. This new-consciousness can influence our conditions; it makes us more and more impersonal; our knowledge, our feelings and our actions all become super-personal. The self transcends the ego-centricity

(g) *The Super Ego* :—

Kuṇḍalinī establishes the sense of the super-ego in us. This super-ego is not the one that emerges by repression in the form of conscience and moral sense; it transcends the Freudean sense of the super-ego and emerges when the conscience is freed from its limitations. When Kuṇḍalinī functions, these natural limitations are removed. Our being stands out in its stature and height, and at times our personality looms large behind the reflected personality or the ego. This super-ego is not one that is dominated by the sense of values, for values are determined by a kind of tension between the higher and the lower impulses of our being, whereas the super-ego is beyond all tension. It appears when all the conflicts, in the subconscious impulses and the self-conscious formulations die out. It implies the overcoming of the natural man with all his natural and divided bents ; a new force which puts aside the discords, the inequilibrium of the instincts, and the conflicts of the self-conscious life. It is a life of perfect rhythm, and widening consciousness, which goes beyond all the earthly impulses or desires. It is the spirit that is beyond our knowledge. The force of Kuṇḍalinī leads us beyond our animal and human limitations and makes us feel the expansive self, to which space and time can form no limitations. This does not give metaphysical insight. It gives an active acquaintance with such a self which sooner or later, becomes intimate with us.

The Tantras maintain different layers of consciousness. The Tantras trace out the link between the subconscious and the super-conscious. This link is ordinarily missed. It is the way to wider consciousness. The psychiatrist is not interested in the study of the subconscient vital layers—the Id of Freud. No doubt, he throws open the vital and psychic being, but his scope is especially limited to study the movement of the vital in the light of the wider consciousness. The psychiatrist throws the light of the super-conscious upon the subconscious to find out the continuity of the conscious life throughout all its scales and grades. When the link is consciously established between the super-conscious and the sub-conscious (both belonging to the unconscious,) the egocentric reference of consciousness is dis-established and its activities are suspended. The direct contact is established with the cosmic consciousness and in place of ego-centricity, a cosmo-centricity is actually felt. This is the super-ego that has its points of reference everywhere. To get direct access to this universal centre of consciousness is the ultimate end of the Kuṇḍalinī Yoga.

The discontinuity between the sub-conscious and the superconscious is obstructive to the still higher evolution, for the whole range of conscious life and its integralness, however thought of, is not a matter of direct experience. And the centralisation of being is not well-established. When the link between the super-conscious and the sub-conscious is well-laid, the whole sweep of our being becomes a matter of direct experience, and the lower centres are infused with the force of the higher. The process of refinement makes them fit vehicles for spiritual expression. The Yoga of Kuṇḍalinī really changes nature fundamentally; the impulses and the impellings lose their personal character. They acquire cosmic meaning.

The Tantras trace out the definite centres wherefrom progressive contact can be established with the centre of cosmic consciousness and which receive and react to the wider forces. These centres are the point of generation and diffusion of psychic force. They have connexion with the definite forces, the vital, the mental, the physical. They exhibit a direct line of connexion with the central force and consciousness ; and naturally when they become psychically active (*i.e.* when the psychic force is generated in these centres) they become highly vibrative, delicately sensitive. The full light of consciousness becomes potent in them which focusses not only the definite forces but also reflects the cosmic life that pulsates there. In fact, the active functioning of these centres immediately introduces us to an aspect of the cosmic life. The movements of these centres enlarge our knowledge of a definite section of cosmic life and fill us with power and force. The rise of the force is, at times dangerous ; for the least retention of the old personality may lead the force into questionable channels. Only the reference to the cosmic life can be helpful to its proper guidance ; when the force of Kuṇḍalinī makes all the centres active and passes through them taking its ultimate rest in the super-conscious expanse, it gets equilibrium. Kuṇḍalinī has its proper centre in the supreme-consciousness. Its operation is stopped in creation, for it is the move of concentration, while Kuṇḍalinī is the force of diffusion and expansion. The higher it goes up in its ascent through the psychic centres the more it acquaints us with all the layers of consciousness. Finally it touches the universal focal point and invests us with the peace that passes understanding.

(*h*) *Cosmic Kuṇḍalinī* :—

The six centres are located thus. The lowest centre, called the *Mulādhāra,* is located at the bottom of spinal cord. Between this and the navel is located the next centre, called the *Svādhiṣṭhāna.* At the navel centre is located the *Maṇipura.* Behind the heart centre is located the *Anāhata.* In the throat is located the Vishudha. Between the eye brows is located the *Ājña cakra.* In the brain is located the *Sahasrāra.* A subtle passage in the form of a luminous canal runs through this passage, and a soothing, delightful current of energy saturates the whole being through these centres. Kuṇḍalinī becomes active through the *Suṣumṇā* and the psychic centres which are represented as so many lotuses "open" and function. They are not operative unless the current of the spiritual force encounters them from the base of the spine. This is called the ascent of force. In its ascent or descent, the force becomes operative through the subtle canal and the psychic centres. The ascent comes with the higher aspirations, and the descent takes place when the force has established its equilibrium in the wide expanse of being. The descent follows the ascent. And it is true in a way for when the force is not operative, it seeks its old mooring. The better truth seems to be this. The force, once it is released, becomes diffused in the wide expanse; its nature is to spread out in the widest stretch of being. It is possible to concentrate and make use of it by the force of will, and move it, through the different vehicles of our being. The Tantras have emphasised the descent of the force, but it becomes possible in some cases, selected for some cosmic purpose. There is an ascent and a descent in the period of discipline and training; it is necessary only to make the force active through the psychic centres. The most significant descent begins when the force concentrates after the completest diffusion for some purpose. The descent fills us with new formative power.

It is neither safe nor possible to make exact location of these centres for they are more psychic than physical. The location is determined by the nerve centres engaged. When for example, the *Ājñācakra* functions, the distinct sensation and force is felt in the mind-brain, when the *Anāhata* is operative the centre round about the heart is agitated, when the *Viśuddhākhya* is active, pressure is felt in the oblongata, when the *sahasrāra* is active, the brain, specially the cerebrum is agitated.

Hindu occultism traces out a correspondence between the five elements and the lower five centres. *Pṛthvī*, the element of earth corresponds to the *Mulādhāra*, the element of water corresponds to *Svādhisṭhāna*, fire to *Maṇipura*, *Vāyu* to *Anāhata*, *Ākāśa* to *Viśuddhākhya*. Beyond the reign of *Viśuddha* opens the subtler planes of Manas, and Buddhi. Manas corresponds to Ājñā Buddhi to the centre located between the Ājñā and the Sahaśrāra. The Sahaśrāra opens out to the overmental and supramental planes. Sahaśrāra, thousand petalled Lotus is the most important centre in as much as lower centres are connected with it and the still higher ethereal over-mental centres take their start from it. In the Tantric texts the Sahaśāra is supposed to be the culminating point of the ascent when all the finest spiritual potencies are located and released. It is the point of the cessation of the functional activity of the finite spirit or consciousness (called Nirvāṇapāda in the Ṣatcakranirūpaṇaṃ).

There is another possibility if the search is persistently followed and does not stop with quietness. The Sahaśrāra opens out vistas of over-mental perception and intuition. Mental ignorance is withdrawn and with its withdrawal there is the momentary abeyance of the functional exercise of the divided consciousness. Here the over-mental consciousness becomes operative, and consciousness functions cosmically and passes into the cosmic dimensions of Being.* Purṇānanda, the author of Ṣaṭcakranirūpaṇaṃ accepts the first course and thinks that the realisation of Integral Awareness is the highest point in spirituality. This naturally is the fruition of the ascent through psychic centres, and in this there is not the demand of passing into the cosmic dimensions of being. When the Kuṇḍalinī reaches the highest point, there is a natural fall in the functional activity of our psychic being and the adept passes into the calm. This is not in the least doubted by those that follow the other course. They want access into the cosmic consciousness, and naturally they avoid entrance into the calm and establish contact with over-mental consciousness by following the subtle luminous path, passing beyond the brain centre and by energising the Cosmic Kuṇḍalinī (Mahā-Kuṇḍalinī) in them.

* The over-mental consciousness becomes active with the stirring of the Cosmic Kuṇḍalinī, called in the Tantras Maha Kuṇḍalinī. The Maha-Kuṇḍalinī is the power that moves the whole world. The power that moves the individual being is Kuṇḍalinī.

The brain has direct contact with the higher layers of being, the over-mental. Indeed it is the path of expanded being, larger consciousness and greater powers. The calm that is reached is due to the cessation of mental ignorance (*Avidyā*) and since the adept is not anxious to pursue further, it gets its highest enlightenment there. The other path pursues through the subtler heavens and may pass into Silence after it has got the cosmic and the super-cosmic experiences. The Śaivas (specially the Kashmere school) follows this path, for they point to be functioning of Mahā-Śakti and para-Śakti beyond Prakṛti (Creative force). Nirvāṇa to them is an experience where the creative Prakṛti of the Sāṁkhya becomes inactive and the higher reaches in the Parā-Śakti and Mahā-Śakti have not been attained. It should be remembered that beyond the Nirvānic level of consciousness the finite-I is dropped and the cosmic-I begins to function. We have seen the different stages of its functioning before. Naturally the adept becomes identified in his consciouness with the super-cosmic reality. This consciousness of identity so long as the thread of individuality is retained is intermittent and not continuous The spiritual aspiration establishes fuller life by overstepping creative dynamism, and by reading the over-mental possibilities. The full fruition of dynamic spirituality is beyond our imagination. At the end effort is made to enjoy the spiritual equilibrium by overstepping the cosmic and the supra-cosmic expression of spirit. It requires a long training to elevate consciousness to this plane, for it implies freedom from the downward clinging of life. When all the obscurities of our being have been withdrawn, then this rare spiritual fruition, the supra-mental life and its felicities can be realised. With the functioning of over-mental centres, the whole being takes a new formation; because of the infusion of the cosmic life and harmony. The higher harmony descends into our divided being and remoulds it in order that the old self may not re-assert itself. The over-mental and the supra-mental dynamism guides our vision and regulates our life. Man does not long suffer from the hesitancy and indecision of the ignorant and divided mind, nor is he guided by intellectual understanding. The spirit becomes fully active and gives unerring guidance. But this is not the neutralisation or depolarisation of the cosmic positive and negative forces. This is practically entering into the mysteries of the universal consciousness by overstepping the finite consciousness. The adept enter into the *Cosmic Kuṇḍalinī i.e.,* the central force of the universe. The Sahaśrāra marks the point above, where the overmental silence can be fully enjoyed and the adept may not feel the call for a still further awakening in the overmental dynamism. If the over-mental silence does not overpower us, the access into the still higher ranges of the over-mental powers are obtained.

The cosmic Kuṇḍalinī gives access to the cosmic powers and the identifiction with them. The finite sense drops, and the adept moves cosmically. Direct contacts with overmental powers are established. Consciousness moves in integral synthesis. It is a rare consummation which can be operative in a few adepts. Ar .ndale makes a distinction between the Caduceus Fire and the Kuṇḍalinī Fire (from the experience of a student. He records the experience) "All he could see was a stream of fire, differently hued, flowing from the root of the spine up into the head, with subtle connections, maintaining ever open channels between the *macro-cosmic forces of which* it is a current. It was very easy to confuse the Caduceus force with the force of Kuṇḍalinī, for there is eternal alliance between them ; and the beginner always tends to perceive sameness before he notices differences. The student concerned had the distinct impression that while the fire of Caduceous offered a way of release, the fire of Kuṇḍalinī offered a way of fulfilment. It seemed as if *Suṣumṇā* with its Idā and Piṅgalā aspects, the Caduceus, were a route of release from confinement within the lower bodies, while the Fire of Kuṇḍalinī is in the nature of a witness-guide to the identity of the larger with the smaller consciousness, (Kuṇḍalinī by C. S. Arundale P. 53-54). This calm indicates the suspension of the activities of the Māyā (Prakṛti of Sāṁkhya) and is the precursor of the unfolding of the dynamic spirituality in the transcendental planes of Sadvidyā, Iśvara, Sadāśiva, Śiva and Parameśvara. There are differences in the spiritual aspects of these orders, the ultimate stage of super-cognition is reached when the concentrations of spirit are all set aside and the cosmic and the supra-cosmic spirituality are overcome in the Transcendence of Śiva-

Śakti. Kashmere Śaivism holds that these stages indicate the progressive refinement of spirit; when it is freed completely from all cosmic concentration, it reaches the highest consummation in Śiva. Concentration is the indication of the working of the Vidyā-Māyā, (the over-mental Māyā) which is still a limitation, not in the individual but in the cosmic sense; the complete transcendence requires the uprooting of the Avidyā as well as the Vidyā-Māyā when the perfect quiescence of the spirit is enjoyed. The functioning of the cosmic Kuṇḍalinī invests with the rarest gifts of full acquaintance with and stability in the cosmic and the Supra-Cosmic heights of existence. The adept is carried on the wings of an ethereal and elastic life-force serene with wisdom and impregnated with delight to the mystery of supreme silence beyond all the fluttering of spirit.

The sensitive can feel the centres overhead and if the consciousness can be retained there, the throbbing of the cosmic life can be distinctly felt. Knowledge and power gradually settle themselves. The adept becomes identified with the divine life. The greatest achievement in this path lies in intimately realising the cosmic will and its formation and purpose in the creation; and the adept, in many cases invites this splendid possibility as more worthy, as it makes him a helpmate in giving a divine shape to the cosmic formations. In response to the cosmic purpose, the adept moves on with the rhythm of cosmic history.

(1) Psychic light, colour and sound:—

The conscious functioning of the psychic introduces

us into a realm not otherwise accessible. The knowledge of light, colour and sound is often neglected as subjective fancies. They are not fancies. They indicate projections into the finer and wider consciousness and its modulations. They are the voiceless voice of the deep, the serene irridiscent light that can shine in the midst of darkness, and the exquisite colours that excite blessed feelings in us. Our mental life reaches a level where it acquires knowledge immediately, without any effect and enters into the realm of radiant forms. All these indeed prove the existence of things and being which do not meet the senses. They open the vaster and the wider fields of concrete existence. The psychic light, sound and colour are mixed up with our spiritual feelings. Advance in spirituality is indicated by the cadence and the rhythm of sound vibrations, by the aura of soft light and by bright but subdued colours. Indeed the spiritual growth is indicated not only in the widening spirit, but also in the brightness of being, its freshness, elasticity, and suppleness. The whole being takes a delicate and attractive form. The psychic deportment leaves an impress upon being which has a silent attraction. These sound, light and colours introduce us to the stretches of subtler knowledge. The Tantras ultimately reduce matter into a set of vibrations. The vibrations of the psychic being are finer than the vibrations of the vital and the physical being, and the sound, light and colour that are experienced with the ascent of Kuṇḍalinī are high in potency and intensive in movement. They are, therefore, subtler and more refined than the kind of vibrations associated with ordinary sounds, lights, colours. Indeed their potency and acceleration are so high that it is not easy to bear them. They reveal a new universe in which our thoughts and emotions are quite different from those that we generally have. A luminous universe opens to us in which thoughts are realised as actual creative forces emitting variegated colours and forms. More properly thought or ideas are reduced to vibrations, psychic or spiritual. The ideal becomes the actual. Ideas become forces; and ideas are expressed as psychic vibrations. The psychic vibrations are not different from the creative ideas. They are ideas set in motion. In psychic life, ideas are not thought out; they are revealed; and the psychic vibrations which they produce are easily seen and sometimes their effects are easily perceived. Ideas suddenly flash out and are immediately projected in the form of colour, light and sound. Each psychic force is associated with such vibrations, and it becomes a source of infinite light and colour and form. The psychic fineness can grow so much that the adept can see immediately through all the planes or strata of subtle existence. Seeing then becomes believing. This mysterious seeing is what the psychic development endows us with. The sound-vibrations are called 'Nāda' and the light vibrations are called 'Vindu'. Next to them is the world of colour and form. They are derivatives out of the light vibrations. In the scale of being the light and the sound vibrations are more original, they are the primary expression of the 'mūlaprakṛti' or 'Śakti'. In the order of ascent these are the last to appear. These vibrations are both creative and redemptive; they have this double function. The creative force is also redemptive; for the identical force is both centric as well as eccentric. The Kuṇḍalinī Yoga releases us from the limitation of the vital-mental being. It gives a unique experience, a new experience.

(j) *Our psychic individuality* :—

Our psychic formation has its uniqueness though it does not become evident unless Kuṇḍalinī be active in us. In actual life the differences in men of genius are due to the functioning of a psychic centre or some centres. Jung mentions two types of psychic characters. Yeats goes deeper and explains the different psychic types, the positive men, the diamonic man, the emotional man, the assertive man, the concrete man, the acquisitive man, by will and the creative mind-will and thought, by the dominance of the one over the other. The Tantras afford a better basis for classification by reference to dominant psychic centres. The uniquenes of individuality is due to the psychic tone of being; The psychic individuality determines the type not by the original endowment but by the powers which it calls forth. Will and the creative mind work under the higher influence and the genius will be judged by the amount of the higher influence it can call forth, by making the psychic active in him. The psychic releases the will and thought from their natural limitations. But the psychic self is not equally developed in all, and the nature of our individuality will depend upon the light and the force emitted from the psychic self. The psychic works with the vital, the mental and the higher mental, and it makes these parts intensely active and luminous. And naturally, therefore, the different types will be determined by the cosmic powers that are invoked and infused in us and by their influencing some parts of our being. The cosmic power may influence will, intelligence, intuition, vitality or even physique, each separately or collectively according to the receptivity and the proneness of our being. This explains the nature and the types of genius. In occult science varieties of types are accepted, because it sees the wondrous possibilities that are hidden in us which can be moved to finer functions. The occultist avoids emphasis upon a dull unanimity in the psychic types, though uniformity in the ideal unfolding is insisted upon. Naturally in the occult science, a hierarchy is conceived according to the psychic capacity and to the assimilation of the cosmic powers. The native individuality which is the making of heredity, innate and acquired tendencies is changed with the functioning of the psychic consciousness and the psychic powers. Every individuality can develop these powers to the extent of establishing a cosmo-centricity in his being and moving under the cosmic inspiration. The Tantras always affiliate our being to such an ideal and practically remove the personal limitations by tracing out the cosmic in our central being. This is indicated in the Tantras as opening of the closed subtle passage in the Suṣumṇā which connects up the two ends in our system. When the two ends meet, we are relieved of our imperfect and undeveloped personality and of the contraries which characterise such life and become aware of our immortal and abiding self. Alcemon, a pupil of Pythogras, thought men died because they could not join these two ends. Their serpent had not its tail in its mouth. We are endowed with a double cone in a bipolar existence which shuts us out from our native existence and immortality. When the poles of existence are linked up by reference to the central being, the bipolar limitation of will and thought are removed ; we achieve the ecstacy of the immeasurable, which cannot be imagined but experienced. The meeting of the two ends has a unique significance and meaning.

Such consummation is naturally preceded by many shades of realisation ; the moment consciousness is made free from the objective reference, it exhibits wider movements unfettered by the seers and their objects. Such power is the power of projection.

Phenomenon like Idio-plasticity or ectoplasm are the invariable fruit of the release of the fine dynamism of being and occasionally occur in spiritual life when our nature becomes greatly elastic. The plasticity of our being increases. It sends forth unconscious ejections or emergences from it. A fine influence scatters through it, when the inner dynamism becomes active under the influence of the mantras. Such ejections are the common experience ; but the Hindu psychiatrist does not lay much emphasis upon such phenomenon, for they are not strictly spiritual. What is seriously attempted is to establish direct contact with grace, which can give knowledge and peace. When the nature is stirred up there is every possibility of calling forth varied powers, including the power of projections, but they may be obstructions to the inner illumination and peace. The path is slippery and the great care is to be taken if one is not to be caught up in the inextricable labyrinth of sub-conscious forces and phenomena and mire of black magic.

CHAPTER XVIII

ŚAKTI, NĀDA, VINDU

The Pratyabhiñjā Hṛdayaṁ has in it "the auspicious supreme Śiva desiring to make manifest the universe which is one with himself first of all shines forth as the undivided chit, as the sunya, undivided void". This being then becomes differentiated into elements and things. The creative ideation starts with *Polarisation.* The polarisations in the initial stage takes the form of Vindu, Nāda and Vīja. The Prapañcasāra Tantra says that the original Vindu (The Parā-Vindu), the supreme light bifurcates into a male (hang) and a female (Sah) principles. The Sāradā Tilaka says Vindu is Śiva, Vīja is Śakti and Nāda is the relation between the two *i.e.,* Nāda is the first concrete stressing of the energy. The Vindu is Śiva and Sakti. The Tantras present two kinds of consciring, an indefinite and a definite formation. The world of definite formation comes at a later stage. The indefinite formation is so called because it does not take any shape or form. It is not the universe of concrete emergences, either of personalities or of definite principles. A stage intervenes between the primordial conscring and definite formation. It is just the stretching of the manifestation when nothing definite emerges, excepting the presentation of the original existence into its specific differences and the consciring of the original entity into will, consciousness and activity. It is intelligible in its specific presentation of the otherwise homogeneity of existence. This original energising becomes the principle of further concrescence which does not belong to the world of emergents. The emergents are concrete formations, the concrescences are not. They are mouldings or formations which take no definiteness or shape. This indefinite consciring continues and takes expression in the form of Nāda. Nāda is the most primitive stirring. In it the consciring appears as the Voiceless Voice (Avyatka Raba) appearing in the initial void. This Voiceless Voice, the Avyakta Raba, is the principle of the uncreated and the undifferentiated sound, not specialised in the form of letters but which through creative activity manifests Śabda and Artha which are its forms. "It is Brahman considered as All-pervading Śabda, integral and undivided, whose substance is Nāda and Vindu" (Vide Page 10 Rāghava Bhatta Commentary Vol. 12, Chapter 1, Sāradā Tilaka). Brahman is initially Aśabda but it conscires into Parā Śabda as distinguished from the aparā Śabda (the usual Śabda). Parā Śabda is super sensuous and is not intelligible to the mind and the senses. The adepts have access to it extreme withdrawnness and unification of consciousness. It is "the stress or spanda in the causal condition of cit (consciousness) and appears as the first manifestation of integral awareness. It cannot be mentalised as it is beyond mind : it is understood as the primitive word revealed in the first stress of consciring.

Vindu is the light, the Cit which appears along with their creative ideation (Sakti) and Nāda is their union. The whole of creation is contained in them for it requires Cit (Consciousness), creative energy and the formative expression of the Nāda. Nāda is the union of Śiva-Śakti. It is the first actual stressing. Nāda is really the initial ideating movement. Naturally this meaning of Nāda is different in its first meaning as the indefinite non-ideating consciring. The Sāradā Tilaka differentiates it as effectual and causal. Anyhow in the initial expression no definite formation takes place; naturally here is the non-ideative situation and expression. This is the aspect of *indeterminate* consciring. This stir cannot long continue; there is in it the seed of concrete expression. When the process of condensation has outgrown the indefiniteness of initial consciring, it takes the form of ideating movement in its most rudimentary form. Here is the definite emergence of sound and its symbols. It is really the Parā Śabda, the supersensuous sound formation, indicative of subtle spiritual ideation and striving as distinguished from mental ideation. It is the concrete stirring of spirit felt and experienced in occult audition. The concentration has no definite focus in a centralised sphere. The process of consciring soon outgrows this stage and passes into concrete formation. Especially a new order of central reference in consciousness emerges out at the indefinite background which becomes the pivot of the creative process. This process of concentration continues from the cosmic self up to the formation of personality in man when the field of reference becomes limited. Their difference rises out of their command over wide or limited field of reference. In spiritual life the experience consciously rises to the verge of the impersonal. In the order of ascent our spiritual experiences pass from the definite to the indefinite, and there is the intermediate experience which enjoys the initial stirring in the placid equilibrium in Śiva. This experience is intensely enjoyable because it has in it the primordial expression and stirring of spirit, formless but not still. It invests with the stillness of peace and with the joy of nebulous conscring. These occasionally occur in spiritual life when our nature becomes greatly elastic.

CHAPTER XIX

COSMIC POWERS AND EMANATIONS

The Tantras evoke the cosmic powers as the right method of fulfilment. They throw open the whole being and trace the movement of the cosmic powers in it and take their help for sure realisation. These powers are spiritually helpful and mould our being by the subtle vibrations they produce. They are really spiritual powers which our normal consciousness can not appraise unless there is deep inspiration. These powers are latent in us, and become active with intense spiritual yearning. The spiritual life is more than the life of understanding, for it has to deal with the unfolding of our being and with the realisation of the divinity that is potential in us. At some stage the divine power becomes active and helps the spiritualisation of our being. The Tantras take the help of the cosmic powers and the cosmic harmonies to make our consciousness active in its subtle expression. This kind of spiritual discipline is unique in the Tantras, the improper understanding of which has been the cause of misjudgement and underrating a noble science and a divine art.

The cosmic powers are to be understood as different from the vital life and its creation. The vital insistences are native urges, they are blind and represent the elemental forces at work. Philosopher speaks of life-force.

The word is indefinite, it may imply the unconscious impelling or the cosmic creative urge. To make the sense definite, the Tantras speak of the cosmic powers as distinguished from the vital forces. The cosmic powers are the expression of the universal spirit in its definite functioning, They are not expression of the *êlan vital* or the universal life-force. Spirit-force is original, life-force is the imperfect expression of it

The cosmic forces are the spirit-force in its cosmic manifestation and cosmic function. They are cosmic emanations, they are over-mental god-heads. They are potent with power, force, and wisdom. They have luminous forms, emitting ethereal vibrations and inspiring quick movements and wide comprehension. They are real cosmic existences, reproductions of the primal power casting light on the path. These emanations are necessary in the initial stage of life in spirit, for they offer the concrete help to individual aspirant. They light up the dark canvass of the soul and throw the distant light on the further levels of evolution.

The primal power takes any number of emanations. These over-mental god-heads are immanent in cosmic functioning, ordering, and shaping the courses of events. They are not our mental creations. These forces have different expressions and manifold function. They are forces of grace, wisdom, love, symmetry and power. The cosmic forces are not creative only, they are also redemptive. The creative forces are different from the redemptive. The redemptive force must produce in us a harmony different from the creative harmony. The creative force is concentrative and the redemptive force is diffusive. Anyhow the uplifting spiritual force produces poise and equilibrium and the amplitude of our being reaches utmost expansion.

The cosmic forces do not stir our being in identical way. They produce different kind of modulations of our being, endowing us with varied occult knowledge and power. The cosmic forces can easily elevate our consciousness from its physical and vital level and can acquaint us with fine expressions on the higher over-mental planes. They cause gentle stirring to evoke various tunes in our psychic being.

The cosmic power is exhibited as creative spirit. It conceives concretely and executes accurately. It exhibits the powers of creation. It is perfect in working out details. It harmonises them in a finished product. It reveals itself as creative symmetry and harmony. When this cosmic force is stirred in us, it infuses us with fine creative energy. The creative forces seize us, and acquaint us with archetypal forms. The mastery over their grouping in a definite form becomes all spontaneous. The whole process becomes effortless, smooth and easy.

It is exhibited as harmony and beauty. The cosmic power stirs in us divine aestheticism, the subtle sense of beauty and harmony. It starts the divine imagination which can trace out the pervading symmetry, in the heart of the universe, be-speaking of it as the urge of fullness and completeness. It is associated with the creative urge and makes things beautiful and movement measured and rhythmical. It is indeed the cosmic power that invests the whole creation with beauty. With its touch the distangled forces of life becomes ordered and life becomes invested with grace and dignity. Here the movement of spirit is soft and delicate revealing the depth of cosmic harmonies evoking cosmic feelings and manifesting the divine order of the whole creation from the minute existence to the exalted heights. The creative symphony goes along with cosmic symmetry and harmony. The harmonies have their individual character. The creative harmony is focussed in a definite setting, creation implies definiteness and order in a concrete situation. In working out the details, it requires infinite patience and power to evoke out an ordered whole from a distangled mass. The other harmony is in its widest commonalty spread throughout the universal order free from all tension experienced in the process of divine creation. It can not bear the least tension and can not manifest itself unless our being has attained the high degree of poise and equilibrium. It has the power of producing that ease and grace of being, when it can have its fullest expression in the divine sympathy immanent in the creative order.

Not is this all. The cosmic urge exhibits itself as the widening force, revealing the immanental sublimities. It is not the measured movement of creative rhythm nor the graceful modulations of beauty and joy; it is the over-powering stillness, the repose and peace of static sublimity. The subtle vibrations of the cosmic force are replaced by its evenness and wideness, where the muteness and the silence are enjoyed more than the dance of life. The cosmic urge takes on itself such modulations as can ultimately pass into the enveloping calm and silence.

Contrary to this, the cosmic power can reveal itself in its height and intensity, in its extreme forcefulness and activity of destroying inertia and barrier and obstruction from the path of realisation. Power and not vastness, activity and not silence, fight against and not compromise with inertia and deficiencies of being and nature, intensiveness and height and not vastness and extensiveness characterise its movement. Dynamic height and sublimity more than static wideness and poise are its invariable effects.

Each has its redeeming power. The redeeming force has its own harmony. It is the harmony of grace carrying onward its charge to Light. It overpowers by its fulfilling or completing urge, making up the deficiencies of nature. When the force of grace seizes us, it does not forsake. It ceaselessly functions until it can invest the soul with divine power, light and knowledge. The creative harmony experiences a tension in the moulding of an obstructive matter, Grace experiences a tension in the moulding of a soul enmeshed in matter.

It is indeed difficult to be in complete touch with and enjoy the continuous impress of the cosmic powers. They make us feel the cosmic movements which the highest stretch of imagination can not even picture. To release the flood gate of energy and to move in the wake of cosmic life and will are fascinating and inspiring ideals of the Tantras. The cosmic powers are invoked for the purpose and the powers can invest us with undreamt of possibilities.

The cosmic powers produce the different kinds of psychic vibrations, creative, illuminative, and redemptive. There are movements of light, grace, power and calm. These powers have been given various names :— Maheśvarī, Mahā-Saraswatī, Mahā-Lakṣmī, Mahā-Kālī, Mahā-Tripurā-Sundarī. Besides these others are mentioned as Kamalā, Tārā, Ṣoraśī, Bhairavī ; but they are more or less active in the same way. They represent definite emanations with distinct harmonies. Infinite shades of harmony are embraced in the cosmic life. Each takes a form impregnated with different tunes. The richness of the Tantric discipline is exhibited when our psychic being is influenced by definite harmonies. They generate rythmic modulations in our being yielding wonderous raptures in the soul. But they all are endowed with three fundamental capacities of generating power, granting redemption, and filling with light and grace.

In fact, the different *Devis* (powers) can be classified into groups according to the psychic force, harmony, and form they generate, though it is held that all the Śaktis are endowed with all kinds of powers. Some represent the power to evoke delightful and beauteous movements, some to stimulate the attractive graces and divine poise, some to move the divine will in us. These are specifications of the different functions of these powers. The Tantrik discipline makes us feel the aroma of divine life, and instils the divine rhythm and beauty in us. The Tantras awaken in our different psychic centres the sleeping divine powers transforming our nature completely.

The Tantras concentrate their efforts on emancipation along with powers. Towards the super-humanisation, the Tantras invoke the supreme Śaktī and also the powers that are located in the different centres of our being. Each centre has a residing power. The psychic centres are the pivots of our being. The invocation of Śakti makes these centres active, and endows us with wide knowledge and occult powers. The Tantras make all the centres active in us. The whole being becomes luminous and transparent. We become fully conscious in every part of our being. The spiritualisation of our being is the supreme art in the Tantras. This is done essentially by the invocation of the supreme Śaktī which lies hidden in us. Invocation is the chief method. It is the effect of right aspiration. Aspiration calls down the spiritual power and establishes it within us. With the invocation the spiritual powers move within us; nothing more is required, if the aspiration is intense. This is the path of supreme dedication and offering of our whole being. The aspiration, of course, should be intense enough to reach and move all the parts of our being. When such aspiration and devotion are wanting, the Tantras invoke the hidden powers by the help of sounds.

It is necessary to distinguish the mental and the over-mental reaches of knowledge. Mind studies facts more by analysis than by synthesis. Even when it makes a synthetic effort, the synthesis is the grouping of the facts obtained by analysis. In the over-mental knowledge there is no effort of the kind, it is more a spontaneous presentation than a construction. A new door of apprehension is opened ; the living reality in its concrete synthesis impresses itself upon us. The cosmic togetherness which such knowledge implies becomes a fact in direct realisation. The limitation of mental construction does not obtain here, at once a freedom is attained from the groping ways of mind, and the sun of the over-mental light lits up the whole universe in its details and in its unification. Even in the presentation of the details there is an infinite richness which is beyond mental grasp. The over-mental knowledge is not a mere cosmic synthesis. The delight of the higher reach in consciousness lies in this expansive knowledge which grasps the totality in a sweep and does not suffer the limitation of mental knowledge by the strenuous process of analysis and synthesis. Naturally the self here enjoys a freedom of grasping facts independent of its presentation through the senses and of reflecting the distant and the near, the seen and the unseen in the same moment. The over-mental knowledge is free then from the logical determinations and logical relations. In the cosmic togetherness the facts of existence are simultaneously presented without the relations which conveyed them in our mental knowledge. It is indeed difficult to convey the over-mental knowledge and its nature in language. But it is certain that over-mental knowledge is supra-personal and supra-relational and the universe that is presented does not lose the details. They are assimilated in a cosmic whole : space, time, loose their individualities, and their moments, they are felt in their unfettered and unrestricted being. Becoming is perceived undivided in time, being undivided in space. This, of course, is still a further step, but at a stage of knowledge before that the impression of a cosmic-togetherness in the expanded space, and an integral becoming in the undivided time is left upon us. With the deepening of such impression, the mental-self and the mental-subject is lost into the enlarged self and subject which reflects the whole in the canvass of the over-mental space and time.

CHAPTER XX

THE WORD AND THE POWER OF SYMBOLS.

The Hindu spiritual Science lays great emphasis upon the Word as representing the divine sapentia expressed in the secret soul of the primal rythm of divine creation. It is the first expression of Divine Wisdom in concrete form and is instrumental to make Divine Life effective in us. The Primal word evokes in us soul-stirring harmonies, Chhandas, in a moment of supreme revelation. With our being etherealised, its definite and indefinite emergences leave their impression upon us. These formations are subtle, and through the occult sense they can be perceived. The Primal Word and the Mantras carry the soul unto the world of harmonies, acquaint it with their absorbing force, their infinite forms and multiple colours. The word is the initial expression, which is condensed into different forms of harmonies and the form of Mantras. Mantras are the expressions of the Word (Parasurāma Kalpa Sutram, 1. 7). Sree Aurobinda in his Ideal spirit of Poetry (Future Poetry) speaks of the mantras as the highest inherent revealing form of poetic thought and expression. What the Vedic poets meant by mantras was an inspired and revealed seeing and visioned thinking, attended by realisation, of some inmost truth of God and Self, man and nature, nature and cosmos, life and thing and thought and experience and deed. It was a thinking that came on the wings of a great soul rhythm, Chhandas.

The Tantras regard the sounds to be original element in creation, and every thing can be resolved to sound and light vibrations. They are uncreate. They are forces at the root of creation. Things are only apparent; the more real is the sound-vibration, and still more real is the dynamism or Śakti. Each sound is a spiritual potency. The sounds produce a marvellous change in our psychic being. Their influence is potent and is demonstrated in spiritual life. They stir the inner spirit. Naturally they reveal a world of primordial a-conceptual forms positively active in introducing us unto a plane of existence endowed with the rhythm of spirit by and all mental formations, potent with deep significance, which can be immediately sensed or felt. Sree Aurobinda says regarding the characterisation of a true mantra, "The sight of the inmost truth must accompany the hearing, the possession of the inmost spirit of it by the mind and its coming home to the soul must accompany or follow immediately upon the rhythmic message of the Word over the mind's Sight of the Truth". (The Future Poetry, Arya page 209).

The spiritual discipline of the Tantras mainly rests upon the power and the potency of the sound-symbols. They unfetter the psychic being from the vital impulses by setting up the spiritual tune of our being and infusing in us the vibrations of spirit. They call forth light and life and remove all the rigidities and darkness of our being. The Tantras have worked out perhaps the most elaborate and accurate scheme of relations between sounds and our psychic feelings and expressions. The scheme is a nice study in occult psychology and its truth and efficacy are a matter of occult experience. Any verification of it through normal experience will be of no use.

The Mantras conceive four stages of the expression of the Word. These stages indicate the concretisation of the Primary sound or word which is called 'Parā-Vāk.' This is really the Word in *its essence*. The 'Maharta Mañjarī' has it 'The Parā-Vāk is inherent in Parameśvara and is revealed in it.' It is beyond all creative expression. It is associated directly with divine Wisdom and is Divine Wisdom. It takes concrete forms which can not be mentally visualised, though they can be psychically envisaged.

The next subtle manifestation is the 'pasyanti-Vāk'. The Vāk is here more concretised, its inherent tendency is to find expression (Vahihprasaramabhyugama-rupatwat). It represents the creative power of the word, (Pasyanti punarchha—Maharta-Mañjari). The *parā* represents the potency, the potency gets definite formation in *Paśyanti*. This stirring is the initial situation. It is the word expressed as *the initial* willing.

The next formation is Madhyamā-Vāk. It is word expressed as *ideation* (Jñāna Śakti). Here the Vāk influences intelligence (Budhivṛtti-pravartymantvat). At the next stage Vāk emerges out in the form of active expression in spoken language. The whole process is the process of emergence of the word in its effectual shaping from the causal and abstract stages. The Kāma-Kalā-Vilās draw a nice distinction between the two stages of expression in the Madhyamā Vāk, the one subtle, the other gross. The gross form is expressed in the nine *Vargas i.e.* the vowels and the consonants (Navavargatma), the other form is expressed in the subtle *Waves of sounds* (Nāda) generally supposed to be nine (Nava Nāda Maya). These are sensed in the depth of meditation. The subtle ideation goes with subtle expression. This is the language of the occultist. Language in its essence is the Worl and before the word expresses itself in spoken language it expresses itself through the stages of willing and ideation. Word is, therefore, the primal force, and willing and ideation are its condensed expression. The Para-Vāk is the initial stirring of consciousness. It is the indefinite stirring of the primal force, which is made definite in the form of active Willing and ideation in the later stage of creative expression. Vāk is *Willing and Ideation,* which are expresed in the form of Vowels and Consonants and then in the form of language.

The Vowels and the Consonants represent some definite expression ; though they apparently have no meaning, for they are not associated with the created things and objects. Certainly they indicate some meaning, but do not indicate any particular thing or being. Their meaning is therefore not to be sought in any thing besides the vibrations and the projective forces which they create. In the Tantras, these are indicated as definite expressions. They are at times personified and classified as definite powers. Indeed they are powers, for the spiritual vibrations affect the definite parts of our being and move the potential spiritual forces. The association of sounds with the sleeping spiritual forces is a common place in Mysticism. The Tantras develop sound-mysticism on experimental basis. These sounds are to be regarded as the spiritual potencies; when properly sensed they will not fail to afford definite expressions. They take consciousness ever beyond the fine mental construction of concepts. Concepts are relational, the sounds produce non-relational idee-forces.

(a) *Types of sounds*

There are different kinds of sounds and vibrations. Their differences are indicated by definite psychic feelings and powers they produce. Some stir up will and its creative potency, some stir up blissful resonance and fill us up with delicate feelings. Some produce the experience of vastness and unbounded expansion. Some invest with calm. Some affect our vital being, some the mental and higher mental being and some the superconscient being. Every one has an expansive force. Every one helps to unearth the sleeping forces of our being. Each helps to push our evolutions to a higher plane of the subtler being. In fact they bring forward the divine nature of man and release him from the dullness and inertia and makes him effective in every way, in knowledge, power and thought. They inspire intuitutive wisdom, move the cosmic will and divine imagination. The Tantras take into account the psychic individuality of each man, prescribe the path of his evolution by ministering unto him the sound-force suiting his psychic nature. The path of evolution is to be traced with rare caution; the disproportion between the force that is generated and the constitution has a terrible effect. To suit the economy of our nature the Tantras conceive many sound-forms. Lesser souls by their clinging to earth consciousness can not generate the mightier force. The spiritual force can not immediately act in cases where the vital satisfaction is sought. The sound force in such cases will stir the vital being to its utmost and after yielding such satisfaction will stir the spiritual force. The Tantras follow the natural bent of being but effect a gentle transformation from within. The sounds-vibrations though they seem to re-awaken the native forces, help to change their direction and character by the slow process of transformation. This way the Tantras produce effectiveness along with transformation. Finally all the native forces of our being are brought under the influence of supreme spirit and are moved by it. The art of the Tantras lie in not rejecting the natural impulses, but to bring them under the guidance of the supreme force which moves them for cosmic purpose. In this only their original character is changed. This regeneration and elevation of nature is the supreme end in the Tantras. A deification of our being is the desideratum.

(b) Sound, Light and Form

Sound vibrations are followed by serene light and radiant forms. They set up a new order of realisation. They produce shades of flashing colours and pillars of light. These colours and light, in addition to the superb delight and exquisite feelings, carry us to a new realm of subtle knowledge in which radiant forms and brighter existences are revealed. It is this which has been the main source of attraction of the Tantrik occultism, for it widens our knowledge by psychic sympathy. A contact and fellowship is established between us and the invisible beings, the denizens of the higher planes which send us help, if their assistance is sought for finer evolution. The different kinds of rhythms attract exalted existences according to the affinity. They explain the specific natures of the sounds symbols and their definite powers. This knowledge is very important. In applied Tantricism, our evolution depends upon the conformity of the sounds to our psychic individuality. The least disagreement between them is positively dangerous for the novitiate. Each sound has its definite colour and form ; each has its effect upon our psychic and mental being. The law of correspondence requires that there should be a harmony between our mental being and the sound vibrations. Many sound-symbols are used to suit the requirement of our nature, and to energise the different forces in our being. When the system is highly attuned, all the latent forces become active ; and every part of our being can be so regulated that in the end the cosmic harmony with which is associated the cosmic knowledge, can be set up in us, affording us with the best expression and the highest evolution of our being. The Tantras give the art how to set up vibrations by particular sounds waking up the definite forces in our being and the cosmic harmony affiliating our aspiration to the transcendent knowledge and bliss.

The sound waves produce astral vibrations. They are radiated in colours and forms. These colours and forms introduce us into a subtler plane of existence beyond ordinary gaze, engrafting us with wider consciousness and greater powers. They are neither physical nor vital nor mental forces. When these forces become active, our mind becomes sensitive to the finer oscillation of the astral creative power. The language of this plane of existence is occult sound, light and colour. Their meanings are expressed in astral forms. The vibrations become so intense that a dream-land is created and the consciousness released from the physical limitation enjoys the architectonic creation of the astral plane. They are different from the architecture of ordinary dreams. Dreams in occult psychology are not always fanciful creations. They are often expressions of a subtler sphere of existence and are indicative of real formations. They are superior to mental formations and mental imageries. They have their origin far beyond in the recesses of our being.

The astral plane resound with the subtle sound vibrations and is aglow with the subtle light currents. Ramifications of light go along with sound-vibrations, and consciousness is lifted from its dense physical-vital-mental cover, and receives and enjoys the light and sound vibrations of intensity and power, floating in empty space. A touch with this world is the real source of all kinds of artistic inspiration. The finest creative impulses emerge. Knowledge becomes essentially a matter of light, sound and form. The forms are the astral imageries, the condensation of sound and light, and is denser than the other two. The aspiring soul leaves the the world of form and enjoys the vibrations of sound and light. Our emotions vary according to our knowledge. They become ethereal and take expression in colours Thought becomes rays of subtle forces, taking shapes in the language of form and colour.

The Mantras, besides moving the psychic and the astral forces, finally resolve themselves to Nāda and Vindu, the primal sound and the primal light. The primal light has the appearance of either of white or of red according to the vibrative frequency of the primal power. The white Vindu is called the Surya (the Sun), the red is called the Soma (the Moon). The former is characterised by a greater equableness, the latter by an intensive frequency. Both radiate serene and soft light. The white symbolises knowledge, the red power. The Kāma-Kalā-Vilās affirms that the white light is Śiva and the red light is Śakti. Their appearance and conscious realisation are possible at the end of the ascent where all concrete formations disappear, leaving behind the primal force, in its original, primordial expression. The Mantra-Śakti does not stop with the exhibition of concrete powers, it expresses its true nature when it passes into the primal light. Every mantra is potent with this possible fruition, which exhibits itself, if its full expression is not interfered with by personal seeking or desire. The Tantras speak of another light, called Agni or the spiritual fire. Fire is purifying. These lights (of Surya, Soma and Agni) represent degrees of spiritual illumination. The rhythm of colours represents the grades of spiritual expression and knowledge.

Mantras are the condensed form of the sound-essences. The one undivided sound essence divides itself into a multiplicity of sounds. So says Natananda-nath in his commentry on the Kāma Kalā Vilās (vide verse 9).

(c) *Varṇamālā. (Garland of Letters)*

In Hindu Mysticism the *Mantras* (the spiritual potent sounds) play an important role ; but the Tantras make a distinction between the Mantras and the Varṇa-mālās. (garland of letters)

A clear distinction is necessary, since the Mantras are also forms of sounds—and their combinations. The Mantras are the sound symbols of some dieties. They produce definite vibrations, which in their intensity take a concrete shape. These are stresses, condensed into definite forms. They originate a meaning and a certain objectivity. The sound vibrations in the

Mantras condense into luminous shape and form endowed with power. Hence in orthodox terminology it is said that the Mantras have their corresponding *devatās* (psychic and spiritual powers). The correspondence between sound and form is true in psychic life. And the best way to accelerate the psychic force is Mantras. The power of concretion is inherent in the Mantra. It must emerge out in some definite shape or form. This force of concretion is not immanent in Varṇamālās. They are also sounds, but not composite sounds; they, therefore, do not modulate in the way in which the Mantras do. Our psychic being is equally affected by both; though the psychic vibrations which they produce are of different intensity and force. The psychic force can take its concrete expression more easily with the Mantras than with Varṇamālās. This distinguishes the one from the other. The Varṇamālās also generate force. They restore additional force to the Mantras. They allow psychic efficiency, harmony and ease. They tune up the psychic being in such a way as it can effectively react to the spiritual forces liberated by the Mantras. The Varṇamālās are called *Mātrikās,* which signify the creative, the ideative and the protective forces. They are reinforcing forces, which make it possible for Mantras to act and be effective quickly. The Mantras are the formative forces, the Varṇamālās are the efficient forces. The Mantras confine us to the world of cosmic vibrations, powers, concrete essences and ideas. They have also the power of transcending these concrete forces, if they are stressed further and if our psychic being is ready to forsake the concrete experience the Mantras create. But the potentialities of Mantras differ. Each has not the identical potentiality. Some are endowed with the power of concretion, others not.

The force and the form of concretion distinguishes the Mantras. The concretions are varied. They represent the kinds of stress which are generated. This concretion of forces is recognised by the Tantras and definite use is made of it. It releases the different lines of psychic force and creates magnetic fields of various extensities.

Mantras affect our whole being. They liberate vital force, produce emotional intensity, quicken up spiritual potencies, and initiate higher mental activities. They cover up over whole psychic, mental and vital being and establish a fine responsiveness and a serene poise in them. They can produce vital and mental intensities, and in some case mental and vital calmness, according to the demand of our being and purpose. They can make our energies active and flow either in the direction of effective contemplation or in the direction of effective expression. Each Mantra has its uniqueness; but as a general truth it can be said that Mantras generate an indrawness and a withdrawness from mentalised habits. They produce a negative and positive result in dispelling the settled convictions and habits of intellect and will and in releasing new forces in life's setting. They act upon our whole being and set a new tuning in it.

The Tantras classify the Mantras according as they produce vibrations in the vital, the mental and the higher mental and spiritual being. The different disciplines and methods laid down in the Tantras originate this way. They are different spiritual paths prescribed according to the needs, requirements, and especially to the psychic and vital make-up of the aspirant. The aspirant with the intensity of the vital being naturally will require a discipline different from the aspirant otherwise developed.

The Tantras arrange and distribute the Vowels and the consonants (these are Varṇamālās) throughout the different centres of the psychic system. They are located at the different parts of the spinal chord. Each centre is represented *as a lotus*. This, no doubt, is symbolic. These centres become active through the force generated by the Varṇamālās and the Mantras. The Varṇamālās are distributed with psychic insight. The Vowels are distributed from throat centre upwards, the consonants are distributed from the heart centre downwards. In psychic science this location may have some meaning and purpose. The psychic centres at the different levels of being generate different kinds of response and feeling according as the different elements are affected. Occult psychology analyses feel-ings, movements and knowledge in this light; it thinks that our vital, mental and psychic being are always affected by the forces of the subtle elements composing our being. These elements are the original forces active in creation (not necessarily material, although always supposed as such, for they are the individuated forms of the original creative force) which cause vital, emotion and mental vibrations.

The physical and the vital forces work with the psychical. The bio-psychical and the physico-psychical constitute the forces at the centres. The Varṇamālās move these forces, and therefore, produce vibrations of different kinds according to the predominant elements of the centres. The elements are the earth, the water, the fire, the air, and the ether (sound). The Hindu psycho-physics links up smell and some form of colour vibration with the earth, taste and some form of colour with the water, energy and some colour with the fire, power and some colour with air, sound with sense of expanse with ether. In fact the Hindu psycho-physics traces intermixture of the original elements, and attributes different psychic qualities to the centres according to the intensity of the vibrations and the composition of the centres. Different forms of enegies are released at the centres by the letters ; and they produce different kinds of psychic vibrations. The Varṇamālās thus originate forces at different centres, each of which has a certain character. Their chief action lies in making us conscious in the every part of our being. It is more important to realise that in mystical life it is more necessary to develop consciousness than to develop power ; when this healthy guidance is not heeded to, the progress on the path is checked. Very often the subtle vibrations of the Varṇamālās produce pleasing sensations, and endow us with powers, which do not allow the detached attitude. The great suppleness and the plasticity of being are felt at every centre. But the highest ascent is not possible unless a supreme withdrawness is evenly maintained throughout. The danger comes with the release of powers as they may attract our attention ignoring the supreme venture. The forces that are released must be gathered up in order that the momentum for higher unfolding can be secured. The least attention to the pleasing sensations and the effecetive powers can only defeat the supreme purpose, freedom from the restricted ways of life. Varṇamālās are to be looked upon as the sources not only of liberating force but also of consciousness — they throw the light of consciousness on the dark canvass of the unconscious. They are originally forces. Whenever the forces move, they focuss the light of consciousness on the centre, fill our whole being with it.

There are mantras which stress beyond special concretions and reach us to the wideness of being and consciousness. All might have the same intensity to vibrate in a way that can touch the fringe of impersonal consciousness. Once the concretions are formed, it is difficult to break them. They give emotional satisfaction as well as awake impersonal consciousness. This is possible when the detachment is evenly kept up and the vibrations become gentle, producing wide feelings. Stages of psychic experience are passed before such consummation can take place. The vital feelings, the emotional stirrings are generally associated with spiritual life ; but they are overcome when the force works in the higher centres. The danger is that in the excess of vital enthusiasm and vital feelings the quest may be lost. Emotional enjoyment can be got over by the spirit of serene calm and detachment. There is the danger of being a prey to the forces of power in Tantricism. And most fall a prey unless there is knowledge and detachment ; full flowering is possible when there is no demand from any part of being. Then the flow of the force is not obstructed and is not kept to restricted expression and satisfaction. The spiritual art, therefore, as indicated in the Varṇamālās, is to keep the continuous and unobstructed unfolding, up to the end. The new life-force that is released invites engrossing attention and the higest end of freedom is possibly missed in the harmony and the music of spirit, if not in emotional excess and in vital intensity. Momentous fruition is sure to emerge, in the form of mental and psychic gifts but even there the spirit of non-attachment is to be retained, otherwise it is not possible to go beyond and transcend the creative order and to enjoy transcendental powers and peace. And therefore, it is necessary to go still beyond where the potency of the Varṇamālās is not even active. There the primal Śakti passes into equilibrium and become one with the transcendent peace. Knowledge and peace are the finest fruits of the spiritual life. The whole art of the Tantras lies in releasing life-force, in redeeming it from the mechanised or intellectualised habits. The mental construction is removed and the spontaneous living is enjoyed. The Tantras give us the secret of this spontaneous living by shutting out the intellectual constructs, and by releasing life-force beyond such constructs. The greater experiences in the process of unfolding are intensely pleasing, but these experiences are not so much important as the spontaneity of spirit, released from the intellectual cobwebs and will-constructs. Ordinarily, the spiritual art in the Tantras is instrumental to the release of the will-power and the vital force. True, they emerge out as life-force is released. But they are soon overcome, when the tension and resistance involved in them are removed as the freedom from ego-constructs is achieved. Though the Tantras are full of spiritual fruitions and experiences of varied kinds—indeed they follow with the ascent of the force through the cadres and the grades of our being—still they emphasise the perfectly deconditioned mental existence and integral awareness. There is in spiritual life this aspiration for a freedom from the mental constructs and this is fulfilled in integral awareness which comes with sponteneous living. This has no reference to the cosmic or supra-cosmic realisations, for they are confined within a focalised consciousness, but integral awareness is beyond it. Consciousness has no reference to anything outside or beyond it. It is integral living free from all tension and conflicts of ideas and values. So long as tension, conflict, ideals, dominate in us, we are after patterns of reality created by intellect, far removed from reality itself which is beyond them and can hardly be achieved when we seek it by the method of discipline. To know this is to free ourselves from the limited creation of intellect or will

To know it is to be one with it *i.e.* to achieve the integral awareness. Cosmic sympathy, cosmic revelation are experiences, indicating the ease and the joy of unfettered life, but the integral awarenes is unique in itself since it is free from all paterns of intellectual and will-construction. It is indeed true to say, as it is often said, that the Tantras emphasise the transcendent creativity and will as the ultimate force of cosmic expression, but it will be hardly true to say that Tantricism is all that. The highest consummation is integral awareness. It can not be achieved, if the highest withdrawness is not achieved, if the forces continue to react, and if the ego-centric reference is not shaken off.

CHAPTER XXI

THE ASCENT AND THE DESCENT

The Varṇamālās are set in the different centres of the psychic self. The Tantras conceive them arranged in the six centres of the psychic system. These centres are described Lotuses. This is perhaps figurative descricption. These lotuses have different numbers of petals, and the Varṇamālās (the whole scale of orthography, vowels and consonants) are supposed to be inscribed on the petals. Normally they remain inactive, for our attention is never directed to them. Nor can it be easily directed. This requires concentration and understanding and above all psychic insight. To many they are more or less illusions. To the few, they are real centres of force, which, if made active, opens the gates to new knowledge. It is seen that the veil of the unconscious can be lifted by moving the Kuṇḍalinī and keeping its flow unobstructed until it connects the two ends of the spinal column. And this is generally done by moving the Varṇamālās to active functioning. When all the centres move in unison and harmony, the clear indication of a wider consciousness is attained. Our knowledge becomes intuitive, feelings serene, and vision unlimited. A new order of experience immediately reveals. This way lies the secret of undreamt of possibilities, provided there is no hindrance because of the inrush of vital insurgence. The fruition takes two forms, the releasing of the psychic body and the releasing of the cosmic consciouness. The second one comes at a higher stage of development where there is nothing to keep the force down. This possibility can not be fully established unless the luminous being of the psychic self forces onward, and unless it can be spontaneously released at our will. The psychic self is a lucent and delightfully vibrative existence charged with frequency and power.

When higher force filters down into the abyss of the subconscient life, it can clear up the obstruction offered by the old habits and ways of the vital and the mental life. Both the ascent and the descent are necessary to be effective in the psychic and the overmental and still higher reaches of consciousness. Generally the Tantras recommend the opening at the lowest end of the spine, supposed to be the centre of Kuṇḍalinī, to be subsequently pushed upwards. The better method appears to be to make it active at the heart-centre and then make the flow upward till it reaches the overmental and the supra-mental beyond the top of the brain and then direct the energy flow downward and put the whole being under its control. There is the instruction in the Tantras given as to the guidance of the force upward and downward by ascending and descending the scale of the Varṇamālās. Some prescribe starting from above and again reversing the process upward, others recommend starting the process from below, and then directing the process again downward. Both the ways are effective. They are to suit the individual convenience according to the nature of its being. In any case, when the whole scale has been successfully traversed, intimations of spirituality become evident. It is then felt that the spirit-force is active everywhere, and it creates electro-magnetic fields round about us. Our being and our surrounding atmosphere become charged with it. At times the stressing of force is intense enough to make us feel the centres as charged. They work at a high degree of frequency. The force should not be evoked for pragmatic purposes. They are too sacred for that. Concentration to these ends can not ease it from life-ends, which, however. are not its great promise. The highest promise comes when the force flows evenly without any guidance or compulsion, for its natural tendency is to allow us the highest gifts of knowledge, wideness, and above all the integral awareness and liberation by depolarisation of life and consciousness. This indeed is its highest privilege ; still the force can be worked in a way which can heighten our personality and can make concrete fruition possible. All this depends upon how do we regulate the forces for 'Bhoga' (the psychic powers and fruitions) or for 'Moksha' (liberation or emancipation). Our progress is an ascent from level to level, and each new ascent starts new inspiration and opens new vistas of much that is still to be released.

In this ascent and descent what is most helpful and encouraging is that an ever-growing conviction seizes our whole being and gives guidance. This conviction takes deep root in us, as soon as the experiences of the diviner forces and its unceasing functioing is obtained. A sure footing is the natural consequence, for then the process emerges out of all doubts, difficulties, uncertainties and becomes spontaneous and attuned to life. It takes long to get away from the masterful insurgence of the crude vital forces, the doubts and refusals of the mind, and to secure the whole-hearted ascent from our total being. The release of the Kuṇḍalinī, and its functioning are not made easy and even possible through the mechanical mental thinking of an ascent or a descent accompanied with a slight effort of attention. What is necessary is the deep conviction in the spiritual destiny and the unconditional surrender to the force and its willing acceptance. When these are neglected, the fruition is eventually frustrated. And, because of this, there must be associated in this process of ascent and descent a fervent aspiration and sincere invoking of the force. Without this the realising act suffers in its intensity and eventually becomes a mechanised habit. Whatever may be the process of spiritual realisation, it should be intensive and integral for a speedier consummation.

The ascent and the descent establish an integral unity in all the parts of our being, and make it work in complete concord and harmony. They remove darkness and rigidities from all the parts of our being in order that the physical, the psychic, the vital and the spiritual can react in an indentical way.

The ascent and the descent make the integral working of our mental-vital system possible and therefore, become the source of the emergence of the integral personality. All the composite parts of our being are brought under the central being and move in unison and harmony. The Yoga establishes this integral self by subsuming the lower under the higher nature and finally bringing them all under the control of the supreme reality and consciousness. The development takes two forms according to the purpose and the ideal fulfilment.

Besides the ultimate consummation in the Calm the Tantras places foward the penumbra of experiences in all the grades of existence which are thrown out in the course of realisation. When the adept ascends into the supra-mental heights, he finds in it grades of ascension, and gradually realises the oneness of being with the divine in its dynamical side. In the complete identification, no difference is left but in partial identification we get greater expression in knowledge, power and bliss. Our being is magnified. It becomes the centre of direct reception. It moves in superhuman ways, and it becomes possible when the spiritual force takes possession of being, fills it with its intensities. Indeed the Tantras show the new path ways of evolution towards complete fulfilment. The Tantras have been interesting this way, and the practical application of the Tantras always hinges upon the removal of the partialities of our nature and upon the expression of the fuller self immanent in us. The Tantras take hold of the spiritual in our being for the finer development, and makes the scientific use of it by following it to the end. This urge gives its indication in blessed and auspicious moments. Life makes intimations of it. The sensitives see it and make use of it.

CHAPTER XXII.

ŚAKTIS AND KALĀS

The Tantras are replete with Śaktis. They are different phases of the principal energy functioning in different capacities. Sometimes the mantras and the form they represent are called Śaktis, sometimes the psychic forces in the different parts of our psycho-physical being are also called Śaktis. These Śaktis are released when the Kuṇḍalini makes its ascent. They are helpful forces. They endow us with the knowledge of the different planes of our psychic existence and even of the wider cosmic existence. Each centre has its individual Śakti. Every centre is modulated by gentle rapturous vibrations which become helpful in reflecting the stratum of existence and in removing the contracting forces, and in establishing light and peace therein. This is the way whereby the Tantras establish the light of spirit in all the parts of being, and finally a spiritual harmony within the whole nature. Nature with her crudities are removed, and a fine emergence in spiritual personality ensues. The vibrations that are set up in our being can effect the environment and establish an atmosphere helpful to the emerged existence.

Śaktis are centred in the principle six *chakras*. The Saradātilaka says "Kuṇḍalini, though it shines brilliant as lightning in the Mūlādhāra of every Jīva, yet it is in the lotuses that she reveals herself and dances in her own joy". When the Kuṇḍalinī makes its ascent and strikes the different centres, it wakes up the force that is immanent there. These forces at the centres (generally called Śaktis) are the specific expression of the primal force in a definite centre. They are active at the different heights of being. Their specific character is indicative of the specific functions they serve. Though the ultimate force is spirit, it takes on it a distinctive feature according to the nature of the centre it energises. Some generate vital force, some emotional modulations, other rhythmic imageries and poetic expression.

Anyhow mantras lift the veil of ignorance from psychic and spiritual being and revives the unbounded consciousness. The Tantras have gone into the detailed description of the forces funtioning at different centres, which are not quite intelligible unless there is acquaintance with the forces. And this direct acquaintance is not possible unless under the pressure of the ascending Kuṇḍalinī these forces are released. The Kuṇḍalini gathers up in intensity as it rises by releasing the vital and the psychic knots and by the widening of consciousness. The Ṣatcakranirupaṇaṃ narrates the different Śaktis and their powers in details. They introduce the procession of light, colours and sounds. They endow us with powers over particular parts of our being and their cosmic counterpart. When the psychic centres become intensively active, the obstructing and the covering forces are removed and the central psychic force becomes active, revealing its correspondence with the cosmic forces. This explains why the Tantric adept acquires super-human powers. Nature yields her obstruction, allowing a free movement and powers to the adept. When the adept passes through the intricate mazes of the released powers and the creative forces, unattached by their charms, possibilities, dignities, then he is in a position to leave aside concrete experiences and formations and attain the undisturbed quietus. The Kuṇḍalinī does not stay constantly in the highest centre in the brain (the place of the Śiva), but makes descent and goes to Mūlādhāra, its original locus. The ascent and the descent then become spontaneous ; when the upward current flows down, it rejuvenates the whole being, reinforces the psychic energies located at the different centres. The adept then moves freely with his cosmic vision and adopts accordingly. This way the limitations of knowledge and adaptations are removed and a superior evolution in being is attained. Knowledge becomes intuitive, will becomes cosmic, and the simplest reactions are all done with the cosmic end in view. It is then natural for an adept in the Tantras, to move towards cosmic ends, and as well to fix himself in the transcendent quietus of being.

The full potentiality of the evolutionary urge has not been actualised. Though the evolutionary urge has found its expression in life and mind, still the superconscient possibilities are not yet fully developed. We are not still acquainted with powers that are active to push the evolution forward. These powers, when awakened and moved to activity, will work towards the greater humanisation of our being by removing the grossness from our nature, and by releasing hidden forces. Evolution at this stage reaches the spiritual level. The emergence of life and mind is a great advance in evolution, but the emergence of spirit is the great demand that is still within us. The Tantras are fully alive to it and therefore, discovers the latent forces in the different centres of being which can make the evolution sure. Some of these forces are in our sub-conscious life, some are in super-conscious life. When these forces become active the veil from the sub-conscious and the super-conscious life are withdrawn. The sub-conscient forces are physical, vital and emotional, the superconscient forces are over-mental and super-mental. The Tantras trace out a correspondence between these forces and the elemental composition of man.

Very few are conscious and actively conscious in vital or physical, sub-mental layers, and in the super-conscient reaches of being, and naturally our consciousness is at a low degree in its functioning and operation. Evolution is hastened when we become conscious in these opposite parts of our being. The Tantras achieve this by introducing harmony in the vital and physical being and making them attuned to the higher being. Without this there may be constant clash, discord and inharmony in our being, which defeat the end.

Nature helps herself here. When harmony is established in any part of our nature, there is the unconscious effort in it to establish it in the whole being. And naturally, when the sleeping forces in any centre are released, its influence work upon the other centres and also makes them active A sympathy runs through. This sympathy makes ascent as well as the descent successful and easy.

When the powers become active in the higher centres, we become cosmically and supercosmically conscious. As the force ascends many kinds of psychic feelings and powers are generated. The ascent is indicated by greater transparence. The highest reach is attained when the Nirvāṇa-Śakti and the Nirvāṇa-Kalā are unfolded and become active in the topmost part of being. The Nirvāṇa-Śakti is the supreme power at the root of the whole creation. It is the primal and initial force. It is full of splendour. The text says that it has the splendour of the million suns. It secretes delight and carries light to the aspirant (Ṣatcakranirupaṇaṃ). Non-attachment is the secret to the Final Peace, non-attachment to the occult powers and even to creative forces which are released as the Kuṇḍalini has its ascent.

Each centre has its own power and expression. The higher forces are more radiant and expressive. They excel more in knowledge than in blissful feelings and effective power. In the Ājñā-cakra the finer will is moved together with the illumined subtler visions. When the force becomes active in the heart centre, it originates cosy feelings and glorious perceptions. The heart is the psychic centre and the psychicasation proceeds therefrom. It emanates its psychic fire that spreads over all the inner parts of our being which become responsive to the gentle occult forces. The vital power is refined and strengthened when the occult force becomes active at the naval centre. Uncommon vital freshness and strength are experienced. The whole being becomes surcharged with a new light and potency. The common effect is everywhere the same, transperence in expression and feeling, elasticity of being, free movement, but with the higher centres, the psychic vibrations become more luminous, soft and expressive.

The scattered vibrations and the moving light are condensed into the mellowed brilliance of pure wisdom. The first vibrative impulse of life with the diffused rays of light emerges out like the scattered rays of the ascending sun on the horizon. The sun of truth sheds its reflections upon the luminous collective being of the aspirant, like the rays of the rising sun upon the gathered snows of the peaks. It gets clothed with its radiance, a pillar of light glowing with the effulgence of spirit.

CHAPTER XXIII

INITIATION

The Tantras speak of Philosophic knowledge as preparatory to spiritual knowledge. The intellectual discipline is not thought enough, it gives a clear understanding, but not always the clarification and the transparence of being without which the revelation of Truth is well neigh impossible. Revelation is relative to the spiritual plasticity of our being. Where receptivity is lacking spiritual discipline can heighten it, where it is already in some form, it can intensify it and make it fit for the direct descent of the powers.

Our being is divided unto itself, and there must be a central aspiration for final illumination. Spiritual life is more than the temporary visitation of spirit. It is the continuous feeling and knowledge of the presence of spirit. This requires a formal initiation. It releases the hidden spirit and liberates our being from the limitations which accumulate round it. The Kashmere Śaivism, however, maintains that *recognition* can independently work out the consciousness of identity. This indeed is the path of Philosophic wisdom, "the eye doctrine" of the occultist. This recognition may be independently possible in the case of rare adepts, who do not require initiation or Dīkṣā. Initiation instils a force into our being. It is "the heart doctrine" of the occultists.

The process of initiation is associated with ceremonials. They are not essential. They are useful in so far as external setting is helpful to inner awakening. Intellectual understanding prepares us mentally, but the psychological complexities are to be eased and removed and this is not possible unless the spiritual initiation gives the inspiration and moulds the life in a way helpful to final illumination. Initiation is really an art of moving the spirit and of making the spirit effective in life. It is really the beginning of a new life, a stirring of a new consciousness. It is the birth of the unborn spirit in man. Where the initiation is effective, it quickens up the life process along with an acquaintance with subtle invisible worlds. The divine aroma of life with secret truths takes possession of the soul. In the case of rare souls free from the complexities of life and endowed with delicate receptivity truth reveals itself, they are the elect.

Initiation is, according to the Nityotsava and the Paraśurama Kalpasutra, of three kinds (1) Śāmbhavī, (2) Śakti, (3) Mantrī. They represent progressive stages of purification. The purification starts with the first one, where the thought of the supreme holy affects favourably the mental being and removes the impurities and inertia of our being. It inculcates some influence and releases some force. The power of thought functions here.

The second form throws a spiritual thrill and sends a current of psychic light throughout the whole being. The spiritual force is felt. It creates a magnetic atmosphere of a new light and new force.

The third acquaints us with the particular spiritual powers as represented in the Mantric-symbol. The psychic and spiritual vibration here gets definite shape and form, and the spiritual consciousness here is more concretised in the beginning. The Tantras lay great emphasis on the mantras which manifest their power at the start in beatific form and subsequently in formless-consciousness. The final realisation is of the primal energy (Śakti) beyond the worlds of determinate formation, beyond space and time. The spiritual initiation stirs the central being and places it in direct contact with spiritual powers. The modulation of being varies with the nature and the form of the force released. These initations are stepping stones to realisation. Naturally the first entrance into the world of determinate formation is followed by the indeterminate consciring.

The nature and form of realisation has already been indicated. The spiritual effort is to be free from the world of mutation and even of personalities. No doubt, the Tantras subscribe to the fellowship in spirituality. It is an exalted experience. The personalities get psychic colouring and appear as luminous and beautiful. Such form of realisation is accepted in Vaiṣṇavic Tantras. Beyond the creative order according to them, is the order of personalities enjoying the fellowship of persons in the supreme God-head. The Śaiva and the Śākta Tantras go beyond and find satisfaction in the super-personal spiritual experience. Personality emerges in the creative order and is not that which is finally supreme. There is urge to trascend the finite personal experiences.

The super-personal experience is associated with the transcendent reality and its supra-temporal expression. Though this emphasis is evident (in the Śaiva and Śākta Tantras) still the concrete spirituality is also marked in them. And that is natural. With the transforming force the person emerges in its psychic luminousity and enjoys its transparent and elastic being. This possibility is in the life of spirit. Spiritual life has infinite shades of expression, concrete and abstract; and it is wisdom, not to be categorised by intellect.

The highest aspiration is reached in identity with the Supreme reality. This experience cuts us of from the personal hold; it allows the supreme consciousness to reveal itself in its identity in being as well as in becoming. The Tantras (the Śākta and the Śaiva) like the Vedānta rise to the height of the spiritualisation by recovering our essence and identity in primal being.

It takes two forms. (1) The complete silence of being in Śiva, where becoming stands in complete equilibrium (becoming is described as *Śānta i.e.* depolarised but the inherent dynamism is there) and has no expression, concrete or abstract. (2) It can also enjoy the expression either in the world of concrete or in the world of abstract formations but at every time maintaining the sense of complete identity with them: they are then looked upon as identical with it. Any how the sense of definite personality is completely dropped. These two aspects are not different. They are identical realisations seen and viewed from two aspects. Here the Śaiva Tantras differ from the Adwaita Vedānta as well as from the Viśiṣṭha-Advaita Vedānta. The one does not recognise becoming in this height of existence, the other retains the individuality of finite experience. Even if the finite experience reaches the height of a cosmic realisation and at times enjoys the cosmic life in its cosmic setting, it does never part with its own self-reference. Freedom means losing its individuality hedged round by egoism and ignorance and its absorbing and assimilating of the cosmic life, where it finds the divine meaning of the cosmic order and its place and purpose therein. The direct contact with the divine implies its transcendence of the limited vision and outlook and its gradual assimilation of the greater life through the divine federation of personalities in society and finally in Civitas dei. Here the life-impulse is serene and quite, expressive and embracive, finally it becomes an offering to and expression in grace.

The Tantric realisation transcends the fine modulation of being in grace and embraces dynamic identification with the root-existence. The felicities of personal spiritual experiences are overcome by the wider possibilities of cosmic being and consciousness. The old self dies and the adept enjoys being and its movement in unfettered expression. Creative emergence is essentially the concentration of the primal reality. Liberation is just the opposite process. It is merging into the ultimate reality. It is *Samabesa i.e.* complete or perfect immersion. Mokṣa is thus decentralisation of the consciousness. It is marked by its freedom from all creative oscillations and its perfect equilibrium in blissful quietus. This blissful quietus comes out last when even the cosmic impelling and life has been over-shadowed in the supra-cosmic dignity. If there is stirring it is also impersonal and transparent. Spiritual life is not so much enjoying as it is becoming and finally being.

The unfettered dynamism is continued even after the personality has been cast off. The withdrawal of the limitation is known as liberation. According to the Vedanta when the limitation is withdrawn, (in liberation), the poise of unfettered being is enjoyed ; but the individual experience is repeated and this continues so long as its momentum (due to commenced Karma) is not exhausted. So long as the momentum works, the individuality is retained. Individuality and identity are naturally incompatiable and these incompatiabilities are reconciled by the extinct of the individual will and efectiveness. The individuality that remains after the attainment of identity is a shadow, its will which constitutes its essence and creates for it a definite world of values and action is lost. The individual can have no effective existence ; it is lost in its wider-self. The construction which pure reason and practical reason sets up has no meaning for the self which has discovered its truer being beyond the dynamic and formative self.

In Tantricism the conflict between the dynamic and the transcendent self is singularly absent, so that when the self transcends the limitation of his individuality imposed on it by ignorance, it attains its dynamic identity and its field of activity and expression becomes